Celebrate Life!

Celebrate Life!

Living to Serve God and Encourage Others
as We Celebrate Life Together

Dee Travis

AMBASSADOR INTERNATIONAL
GREENVILLE, SOUTH CAROLINA & BELFAST, NORTHERN IRELAND

www.ambassador-international.com

Celebrate Life!
Living to Serve God and Encourage Others as We Celebrate Life Together

ISBN: 978-1-62020-531-0
eISBN: 978-1-62020-456-6

Cover Design and Page Layout by Hannah Nichols
eBook Conversion by Anna Riebe Raats

AMBASSADOR INTERNATIONAL
Emerald House
427 Wade Hampton Blvd.
Greenville, SC 29609, USA
www.ambassador-international.com

AMBASSADOR BOOKS
The Mount
2 Woodstock Link
Belfast, BT6 8DD, Northern Ireland, UK
www.ambassadormedia.co.uk

The colophon is a trademark of Ambassador

This book is in memory of and dedicated to my dear and treasured friend Lynne Reeves. You were such an encouragement to me as we worked together writing our first two books. I cherish the fun memories we made as we were writing, especially the time we were in my living room and a mouse ran across the floor in front of us! We both screamed and jumped up into our chairs. Then we couldn't stop laughing! We took advantage of each chance we could get together and work. One week we worked on writing during the county fair as the kids were busy with their projects and horses. One of my sweetest memories, though, is at your kitchen table drinking your homemade lemonade! It was hard to do this one without you, and I put it off for a couple of years, but I know you are glad I didn't give up. You showed me that God is in the details. We learned so much together! I miss you. I am thankful for the good times we shared together as friends! See you soon.

In memory of Lynne Laurine Reeves, 1961-2009

INTRODUCTION

Every day is a gift that we have been given, and that's something to celebrate! God blesses us daily with so many good things. My desire in writing this book is to encourage you to celebrate those good things with your mate, your children, your church family, and your friends. Hopefully these ideas will help you, and even maybe spark a few ideas of your own!

God has given me a wonderful soul mate to celebrate life with. The saying "Come grow old with me, the best is yet to be" is so true. I have only just begun to realize that. Make each day special for your mate by doing the little extras that let them know you love and care for them. Take that evening walk together. Men, check out her honey-do list. Plan a weekend getaway together. Say "I love you" every day!

Children are a heritage of the Lord (Psalm 127:3a) . . . and so much fun. They love to celebrate! Sometimes our lives as parents and grandparents can be so busy that we need to make sure we spend time with the children God has blessed us with. We can show them that God is in the details, the little things in life all around us that are so easily overlooked in our hectic lives. Plan a campout, enjoy a snow day, or just have a fun family night together. They grow up too fast. Believe me!

Celebrating life with our church family is such a good way to encourage and strengthen each other as believers in our faith. Plan to get together with others to find out what is happening in their lives. Laugh out loud with each other. Cry with each other and be there to listen. Cuddle someone's baby. Listen to an older person talk about the good old days. Celebrate the good things God is doing in the life of your church.

Friends are the best. You can be yourself around your friends. Plan fun activities you can do with your friends. Make some memories you will treasure for years to come. Get together and make homemade ice cream and fresh baked pie! Plan an evening to carve pumpkins together, roast hotdogs, and go on a country hayride. You know you want to, and here are some great ideas, so just do it!

Maybe you really don't feel like celebrating. Maybe life doesn't seem all that grand. It is hard to celebrate life if you don't have life—true life in Christ. There is hope. God offers new life, abundant life through His Son Jesus Christ. John 3:16 says, "For God so loved the world that he gave his only begotten Son, that whosoever believeth in him should not perish but have everlasting life." You can know it in your head, but you need to believe it in your heart. It is simply faith in Christ alone and what He has done for us.

Romans 6:23 says, "For the wages of sin is death but the gift of God is eternal life through Christ Jesus our Lord." When Jesus died on the cross, He took the punishment for our sin. He conquered death and rose to life. He offers us the free gift of eternal life with Him in heaven one day. All we have to do is receive that gift. Ephesians 2:8–9 tell us that "For it is by grace you have been saved through faith—and this is not from yourselves—it is the gift of God. Not by works, so that no one can boast."

Forever in heaven one day with Him. Now that is something to celebrate!

I hope this book encourages you to draw close to God and also to those people He has put in your life. It might take a little extra work on your part, but it will be worth it! God is always good, and you are always loved. Every day is a gift, and we get to choose how we live it. Let's celebrate life!

CONTENTS

Celebrating Life with Your Church Family

Celebrating Life with Your Friends

Celebrating Life
with Your Mate

DON'T FORGET THE PURSUIT ONCE you are married. God is constantly pursuing us and drawing us to Himself because He loves us and wants to spend time with us. He is our example to keep pursuing the one you love!

1 Cor. 14:1 Pursue love!

AFTERNOON GETAWAY

Theme: Take time to stop, look, and listen to each other.
Enjoy God's creation around you.

Verses to share and meditate on:

Psalm 19:1–3, *The heavens declare the glory of God; the skies proclaim the work of his hands. Day after day they pour forth speech; night after night they reveal knowledge. They have no speech, they use no words; no sound is heard from them.*

Genesis 1:1

Psalm 8:1

Psalm 146:5–6

Romans 1:19–20

Nehemiah 9:6

Isaiah 45:12

Psalm 135:5–7

Plan some time to go to a quiet place away from the hustle and bustle of jobs or children. Talk and listen to each other about your individual needs and things that are happening in each of your lives.

Make sure you find a place that is relaxing, such as a lake or park. Hold hands and enjoy each other's company as you listen and look at God's creation around you.

Take lounge chairs or a blanket to stretch out on. Bask in the warmth of the sun and in each other.

If you are near the zoo, go and watch the animals as you walk and talk to each other.

If the weather is cold, you can still go to a park and sit in the car and talk and reflect as you enjoy God's creation around you. Maybe there will be some ducks or geese on the lake or a deer or two walking through the trees. Bring birdseed to feed to the birds and squirrels. Take a quick, brisk walk in the snow.

Even if it's only for an hour or over your lunch break, plan ahead and do it!!

Wives: Pack a picnic lunch or snack with something to drink. Think of special ways to impress your husband, like bringing him his favorite candy bar or piece of pie or cake. Let him know you are still "sweet on him."

Husbands: Wrap a small gift or buy her flowers to give her to show her how much you care. Even a small inexpensive gift will make her feel loved and very special. Just let her know it is wonderful spending a few minutes together on your afternoon getaway.

RECIPES:

CHOCOLATE PRALINE LAYER CAKE
Cake:

- ½ cup butter or margarine
- ¼ cup whipping cream
- 1 cup firmly packed brown sugar

- ¾ cup coarsely chopped pecans
- 1 devil's food cake mix
- 1¼ cups water
- ⅓ cup oil
- 3 eggs

Topping:

- 1¾ cups whipping cream
- ¼ cup powdered sugar
- ¼ tsp vanilla
- 16 pecan halves, if desired
- 16 chocolate curls, if desired

Directions:

Heat oven to 325°F. In small, heavy saucepan, combine butter, ¼ cup whipping cream, and brown sugar. Cook over low heat just until butter is melted, stirring occasionally. Pour into two 8- or 9-inch round cake pans; sprinkle evenly with chopped pecans.

In large bowl, combine cake mix, water, oil, and eggs; beat at low speed until moistened. Beat 2 minutes at medium speed. Carefully spoon batter over pecan mixture.

Bake at 325°F for 35-45 minutes or until cake springs back when touched lightly in center. Cool 5 minutes; remove from pans. Cool 1 hour or until completely cooled.

In small bowl, beat 1¾ cups whipping cream until soft peaks form. Add powdered sugar and vanilla; beat until stiff peaks form.

To assemble cake, place 1 layer on serving plate, praline side up. Spread with half of whipped cream. Top with second layer, praline side up; spread top with remaining whipped cream. Garnish with whole pecans and chocolate curls. Store in refrigerator.

FRESH STRAWBERRY PIE

Crust:

- ¾ cup flour
- ¼ cup butter Crisco™
- ⅛ cup cold milk

Cut the flour and Crisco together until crumbly. Stir in cold milk until dough forms a ball. Roll out on a floured surface and place in a 9-inch pie pan.

Filling:

- 3 pints (6 cups) fresh strawberries
- 1 cup sugar
- 3 Tbsps cornstarch
- ½ cup water
- 4-5 drops red food color, if desired

Topping:

- 1 cup sweetened whipped cream

Directions:

Heat oven to 400°F. Bake pie crust for 8 to 10 minutes or until golden around edges. Cool completely on cooling rack, about 15 minutes.

Meanwhile, in small bowl, crush enough strawberries to make 1 cup. In 2-quart saucepan, mix sugar and cornstarch; stir in crushed strawberries and water. Cook, stirring constantly, until mixture boils and thickens. If desired, stir in food color. Cool completely, about 30 minutes.

Place remaining strawberries, whole or sliced, in cooled baked shell. Pour cooked strawberry mixture evenly over berries. Refrigerate until set, about 3 hours, before serving.

Just before serving, top pie with sweetened whipped cream. Cover and refrigerate any remaining pie.

EARLY MORNING MOMENTS

Theme: Walking and talking in step with each other and with God.

Verses to share and meditate on:

1 John 1:7, *But if we walk in the light, as he is in the light, we have fellowship with one another, and the blood of Jesus, his Son, purifies us from all sin.*

Isaiah 40:31

Psalm 89:15

James 1:19

Proverbs 8:6

Proverbs 16:24

Colossians 4:6

Plan an early morning walk with your sweetie. Find a walking or hiking trail or maybe even a country road and enjoy the brisk freshness of the early morning. If you rise up in time, you could even watch the sun come up! If you have small children and can't get far away from the house, just take a walk around it a few times. Or find a spot in the yard to sit together and watch the sunrise. Make it a date at least once a month. What a wonderful way to start your day together with each other and with God as you see His handiwork and design unfold around you. As you walk, talk about things you see and what lies ahead in your day.

Wives: Tell your husband how much you enjoy spending this special time with just him.

Husbands: If you see a flower on the way, pick it just for her!

When you are done with your early walk, go out for breakfast together, find a great coffee bar, or enjoy a special coffee or breakfast at home. Sit and talk about God's design for your lives. Have some early moments together with God. Read Proverbs 3:5–6 and talk about how God guides our paths. Be a good listener. Give your full attention to what your spouse has to say. Reflect on how God brought your paths together as husband and wife. His plans are perfect, and He is always there to guide us as a couple and keep our "walking" paths straight.

RECIPES:

EGG CASSEROLE

- 12 eggs
- ½ cup flour
- 1 tsp baking powder
- 2 cups cottage cheese
- ¼ cup melted margarine
- 1 lb. diced ham
- 1 lb. Italian blend cheese

Directions:

Spray a 9x9 pan with cooking spray. Add meat and cheeses to the bottom of the pan. Whip together the eggs, flour, baking powder, and melted margarine. Pour over the top and bake at 350°F for 1 hour. *Serves 6 to 8.*

MUFFINS:

POPPY SEED MUFFINS

- 3 eggs
- 2½ cups white sugar
- 1⅛ cups vegetable oil
- 1½ cups milk
- 1½ tsps salt
- 1½ tsps baking powder
- 1½ Tbsps poppy seeds
- 1½ tsps vanilla extract
- 1½ tsps almond extract
- 3 cups all-purpose flour
- ¾ cup white sugar
- ¼ cup orange juice
- ½ tsp vanilla extract
- ½ tsp almond extract
- 2 tsps butter, melted

Directions:

Beat together the eggs, 2½ cups white sugar, and vegetable oil. Add in milk, salt, baking powder, poppy seeds, vanilla, almond flavoring, and flour. Mix well.

Bake in paper lined muffin cups (filled ¾ full) or 3 small greased loaf pans at 350°F for 15-20 minutes for muffins and 50-60 minutes for loaves. The tops should be browned and a toothpick inserted in the center should come out clean.

Remove muffins as soon as you can while still warm/hot and dunk tops into glaze. Turn right side up and cool on a cookie rack. With loaves, just pour the glaze evenly over the three loaves while still in pans. Let cool and remove from pans. Yes, it is a little messy, but it is really good. *Makes 12 to 18 muffins.*

To Make Glaze: In a saucepan over low heat, combine ¾ cup sugar, orange juice, ½ tsp vanilla, ½ tsp almond flavoring and 2 tsps melted butter. Warm in pan until the sugar is dissolved. Pour over loaf pans or dunk muffin tops into glaze when cooled to room temperature.

BLUEBERRY MUFFINS

- ½ cup unsalted butter
- 1¼ cups white sugar
- ½ tsp salt
- 2 eggs
- 2 cups all-purpose flour, divided
- 2 tsps baking powder
- ½ cup buttermilk
- 1 pint fresh blueberries—rinsed, drained, and patted dry
- 2 Tbsp white sugar

Directions:

Position rack in the middle of oven. Preheat oven to 375°F. Spray the top of a muffin pan with non-stick coating, and line with paper liners.

In a large bowl, cream together the butter, 1¼ cups sugar, and salt until light and fluffy. Beat in the eggs one at a time. Mix together 1¾ cup of the flour and baking powder. Beat in the flour mixture alternately with the buttermilk, mixing just until incorporated. Crush ¼ of the blueberries and stir into the batter. Mix the rest of the whole blueberries with the remaining ¼ cup of the flour and fold into the batter. Scoop into muffin cups. Sprinkle tops lightly with sugar. Bake in preheated oven for 30 minutes or until golden brown and tops spring back when lightly tapped. *Makes 12 muffins*

PUMPKIN CHOCOLATE CHIP MUFFINS

- ¾ cup white sugar
- ¼ cup vegetable oil
- 2 eggs
- ¾ cup canned pumpkin
- ¼ cup water
- 1½ cups all-purpose flour
- ¾ tsp baking powder
- ½ tsp baking soda
- ¼ tsp ground cloves
- ½ tsp ground cinnamon
- ¼ tsp salt
- ¼ tsp ground nutmeg
- ½ cup semi-sweet chocolate chips

Directions:

Preheat the oven to 400°F. Grease and flour muffin pan or use paper liners.

Mix sugar, oil, eggs. Add pumpkin and water. In separate bowl, mix together the baking flour, baking soda, baking powder, spices, and salt. Add wet mixture and stir in chocolate chips.

Fill muffin cups ⅔ full with batter. Bake in preheated oven for 20 to 25 minutes. *Makes 1 dozen small muffins*

BANANA CHOCOLATE CHIP MUFFINS

- 1 egg
- 3 cup vegetable oil
- ¾ cup sugar
- 3 medium ripe bananas, mashed
- 2 cups flour
- 2 cup oatmeal
- 1 tsp baking powder
- 1 tsp baking soda
- 2 tsp salt
- ¾ cup miniature semi-sweet chocolate chips

Directions:

Beat egg, oil, and sugar until smooth. Stir in bananas. Combine dry ingredients and stir into the banana mixture until moistened. Stir in chocolate chips. Fill greased muffin cups ¾ full. Bake at 375°F for 18-20 minutes or until muffins test done. *Makes 1 dozen.*

WARM HEARTS

Theme: Even when it is cold and snowy outside, you can be cuddly cozy inside as you take time to relax in the warmth of each other's company.

Verses to share and meditate on:

Psalm 51:7, *Cleanse me with hyssop, and I will be clean; wash me, and I will be whiter than snow.*

Psalm 74:17
Psalm 139:13–16
Psalm 147:16
Isaiah 1:18
Job 37:6

Find a great secluded cabin in the woods that has a fireplace or at least a spot where you can build a campfire to cuddle up together. If you can't have a campfire, just place lit candles in the snow for a romantic effect. If your budget allows, rent a cabin with an outside hot tub where a blanket of snow surrounds you as you relax in the soothing warm water. Stars and moonlight will make for the perfect evening!

Read, reflect, and relax!

Enjoy reading together from the book of Song of Solomon in the Bible. It is a very romantic love story. Try reading it from a different version than you may have in the past.

No television is allowed! Play a game of checkers, chess, dominoes, or Sorry together.

Go for a moonlit walk in the snow or find a good place to go sledding down a hill together. Learn to ice skate! Isn't there something fun and romantic about falling down into each other's arms? Or maybe you could just build a snowman together (in honor of the kids)!

Once inside, enjoy a steamy hot chocolate together and munch on a big bowl of popcorn. Talk about the beauty of the snow and how God makes the snow in His storehouses. Isaiah says God can take away our sin and make us whiter than snow. Since every snowflake is unique and special with no two snowflakes alike, share with your spouse what you think is unique about them and why that makes them special to you.

RECIPES:

HOT CHOCOLATE

- ½ cup sugar
- ¼ cup cocoa
- Dash of salt
- ⅓ cup hot water
- 4 cups (1 qt.) milk
- ¾ tsp vanilla extract
- Miniature marshmallows or sweetened whipped cream

Directions:

Stir together sugar, cocoa, and salt in medium saucepan; stir in water. Cook over medium heat, stirring constantly, until mixture comes to a boil. Boil and stir 2 minutes. Add milk; stirring constantly, and heat to serving temperature. Do not allow it to return to a boil.

Remove from heat; add vanilla. Beat with rotary beater or whisk until foamy. Serve topped with marshmallows or whipped cream, if desired.

HOMEMADE CHAI TEA LATTE

- 2 cups water
- 2 black tea bags
- 2 whole cloves
- 1 tsp ground cinnamon
- ½ tsp ground ginger
- ½ tsp cardamom
- ½ tsp ground nutmeg
- ⅛ tsp ground allspice
- 2 Tbsp pure maple syrup

Latte:

- ½ cup chai tea (recipe above)
- ¾ cup whole milk
- 1 Tbsp pure maple syrup
- Pinch of ground cinnamon

Directions:

For the chai tea: In a medium-sized saucepan, bring the water and spices to a boil. Whisk the spices in the water. Once the water reaches a boil, turn off the heat and allow the spices to steep in the water for 5 minutes. After 5 minutes, turn the heat back on and add the black tea bag and maple syrup. Return to a slight boil (the goal is a hot liquid for steeping). Once boiling, turn off the heat. Allow the tea bags to steep in the water and spices for 5 minutes. Remove the tea bags and strain the tea through a fine mesh sieve. Reserve ½ cup of chai tea for the latte. Store the rest of the chai tea in the fridge up to two weeks for freshness.

For the latte: In a medium-size saucepan, bring the milk, maple syrup, and pinch of cinnamon to a slight boil (the sides of the milk will begin to bubble), stirring often. Once the sides of the milk begin to bubble, remove the pan from heat. Using an immersion blender (this is the trick to a frothy homemade latte), blend the milk until it's frothy.

Pour ½ cup of chai tea in a mug. Slowly add the warm, frothy milk to the tea. Sprinkle the top of the chai latte with an extra pinch of cinnamon, if desired. Serve warm.

MONSTER MUNCH

- 1 package almond bark (1 lb)
- 12 cups popped popcorn
- 1 cup candy corn
- 1 cup dry-roasted, salted peanuts
- ½ cup Reese's Pieces™

Directions:

Pop popcorn and place in a large bowl. Much larger than you think you need. The largest you have. It will make mixing easier! Pour peanuts, candy corn, and Reese's Pieces on top. Take a large knife and break up almond bark. Melt according to package directions. Break it up and microwave it in intervals until smooth and melted.

Pour over popcorn mixture.

Stir until everything is well coated and then spread out onto waxed paper, parchment, or foil. Let sit until completely dry and then break up into clumps.

CRISPIX™ CRUNCH

- 1 cup butter or margarine
- 2 cups brown sugar
- ¾ cup light corn syrup
- ½ tsp baking soda
- 1 box Crispix cereal

Directions:

Bring butter, brown sugar, and corn syrup to a boil. Boil 2 minutes. Remove from heat and add baking soda. (It will foam.)

Put the cereal in a large bowl and pour the boiled mixture over the cereal and stir to coat.

Microwave 1 minute and then stir.

Repeat three times.

Pour out onto waxed paper. Cool.

SUGARED PECANS

- 1 lb pecans
- 1 egg white
- 1 tsp water
- ½ cup sugar
- 2 tsps cinnamon
- 2 tsps salt

Directions:

Mix eggs whites and water together with fork. Add pecans and tumble well. Mix sugar, salt, and cinnamon. Add to pecans and tumble again. Spread pecans on cookie sheet in a single layer. Bake 350°F for 30 minutes, stirring evenly every 10 minutes. Cool on waxed paper.

CANDLELIGHT FOR "TWO"

Theme: Keep the flame burning bright in your marriage. We need to be a shining light to other couples so they will see God working in our lives and in our marriage.

Verses to share and meditate on:

Matthew 5:16, *In the same way, let your light shine before others, that they may see your good deeds and glorify your Father in heaven.*

Exodus 13:21

Psalm 29:7

Psalm 119:105

Isaiah 60:1

Ephesians 5:8

1 John 1:7

Plan your special day around the number "two." The verse in Exodus says the two shall become one. Call ahead to make reservations for two and ask for two candles on your table.

Wife: Call your hubby at two in the afternoon that day and tell him how excited you are about your date night. Let him know you are looking forward to a night together with just the two of you!

Husband: Stop by the florist and buy her two roses and bring them home to her. Surprise seems to spark the fires of romance.

Write out Matthew 19:5 (For this cause shall a man leave his father and mother, and shall cleave to his wife; and the two shall become one) on a card to remind your wife that she is the one for you. Place two pieces of chocolate candy on her pillow before you leave for the restaurant. Her heart will melt knowing you did such a sweet thing.

Over your candlelight dinner, talk about old times and what sparked your interest in each other in the first place. Reminisce about how you met or where you went on your first date. Hold her hand. Play footsie with him. Wink at her once in a while during the evening. See if you both can remember that first kiss or that moment in time when you knew the other was the one you wanted to spend the rest of your life with.

Think of other couples who might be close to you, who are watching you as an example. Think of ways to let the light of your marriage shine in ways that you might be of help to others.

Above all be thankful to God that He has brought the two of you together and with Him the flame will not go out in your marriage.

RECIPES:

CHOCOLATE FONDUE

- ¾ cup heavy whipping cream, reserve ¼ cup to thin if fondue begins to thicken
- 4 bittersweet chocolate bars, chopped, 3½ ounces each
- ¼ cup finely chopped hazelnuts or almonds, optional

Suggested things to dip:

- Hazelnut or almond biscotti
- Salted pretzel sticks
- Cubed pound cake
- Sliced bananas
- Stem strawberries
- Sectioned navel oranges
- Ripe, fresh, diced pineapple

Directions:

Heat ½ cup cream in a heavy sauce pot over moderate heat until cream comes to a low boil. Remove the pan from the heat and add chocolate. Let the chocolate stand in hot cream 3 - 5 minutes to soften. Then whisk chocolate together with the cream. Stir in chopped nuts and transfer the fondue to a fondue pot or set the mixing bowl on a rack above a small lit candle. If fondue becomes too thick, stir in reserved cream, 1 Tbsp at a time, to desired consistency. Arrange your favorite things to dip in piles on a platter alongside chocolate fondue with fondue forks, bamboo skewers, or seafood forks as utensils for dipping.

CHEESE FONDUE

- 1 clove of garlic, cut in half
- 2 cups half & half
- 1 Tbsp Worcestershire sauce
- 2 tsp dry mustard
- 1½ lb mild cheddar cheese, shredded
- 3 Tbsp flour
- Salt and pepper

Dippers:

- Bread
- Cooked ham
- Cooked shrimp
- Steamed vegetables

Directions:

Rub garlic halves inside the fondue pot. Discard when done. Pour the cream and Worcestershire sauce into the cheese fondue pot and light the burner. Warm up the cream mixture without boiling, and then mix in the mustard. Mix the cheese with the flour, and then add to the pot, one handful at a time. Let the cheese melt prior to adding more cheese. With a wooden spoon, mix well. Add salt and pepper to taste.

Dip your pieces of bread and other dippers into this delicious cheddar fondue recipe. I recommend rye bread, French baguette, cooked shrimp, cooked ham, steamed broccoli, and steamed cauliflower.

A RELAXING NIGHT ON THE TOWN

Theme: Make plans to spend on evening in another town or somewhere you can make the night special by doing something you don't usually do.

Verses to share and meditate on:

Psalm 62:1, *Truly my soul finds rest in God; my salvation comes from him.*

Hebrews 4:9–10

Genesis 2:2

Exodus 33:14

Psalm 23:1–3

Psalm 37:7

Matthew 11:28

This is a fun getaway where there are no pressures or time schedules to meet. Relax and enjoy a change of scenery. What about treating your wife to that musical or play she would like to go to? Or maybe there is a ballgame your husband never has time to fit in his schedule.

Check to see if there are carriage rides in town. That's probably something you don't usually do and would be relaxing and romantic.

Maybe you could just go browsing at the mall in stores you normally don't take time to visit. Try an art gallery. As you look at different paintings, hold hands and pick out those that are your favorites. It doesn't hurt to dream! Go to one of the large bookstores and browse through each section. Then sip a hot cappuccino or latte together.

If you can, spend the night at a motel so you can catch up on some cuddling and rest by sleeping in the next morning! Do something else you probably don't usually do, like ordering breakfast and eating it in bed.

Spend part of your morning reflecting on God's promises to us. His promises do include that He will give us rest. We just need to draw away for a while. God set the example of rest for us. Rest in these promises of God.

> He gives eternal life. John 3:16
>
> He will never leave us. Hebrews 13:5
>
> He forgives. 1 John 1:9
>
> He gives us peace. Romans 5:1
>
> He supplies our needs. Philippians 4:19
>
> Nothing can separate us. Romans 8:38–39

Think about these promises God made to us and then think about the promises you made to each other and to God in your wedding vows. Renew those promises!

RECIPES:

RELAXING TEA

- 1 tea bag
- 1 cup boiling water

- 1 cinnamon stick
- 1 strip orange zest, 1-inch wide
- 1 tsp honey

Directions:
Put the tea bag in a cup and add the boiling water. Add the cinnamon stick and orange zest and let steep for 5 minutes. Remove the tea bag, cinnamon stick, and orange zest, and stir in the honey.

SOOTHING SPICED MILK

- 1 cup milk
- 1 pinch ground cardamom
- 1 pinch ground nutmeg

Directions:
Put the milk in a small saucepan and heat over low heat until warm. Pour into a cup, add the spices, and stir to combine.

WARM APRICOT SMOOTHIE
This is a nourishing, relaxing drink.

- ⅓ cup dried apricots
- 1 cup water
- ¾ cup milk
- 1 pinch ground ginger
- 1 tsp honey, or to taste

Directions:
In a small saucepan, combine the dried apricots and water. Bring to a boil, reduce heat, cover, and simmer for 10 minutes; let cool slightly. In a small saucepan, heat the milk until bubbles

form around the edge of the pan. In a blender, combine the apricots and their liquid, the milk, ginger, and honey. Process until smooth and drink warm.

MELON-BERRY CRUSH

This summery drink is very refreshing. Strawberries have calming properties.

- 1½ cups chopped and seeded watermelon flesh
- ¼ cantaloupe peeled, seeded, and chopped
- 1 cup hulled fresh, or thawed from frozen, strawberries
- Ice cubes

Directions:

In a blender, combine all the fruits and process until smooth. Serve immediately over ice.

SOOTHING CITRUS ICED TEA

- 1 lemon balm tea bag
- 1 cup boiling water
- 3-4 ice cubes
- Juice of 1 large orange
- 6 fresh mint leaves, finely chopped

Directions:

Put the lemon balm tea bag in a cup and add the boiling water. Let steep for 10 minutes before removing the tea bag. Refrigerate the tea until chilled, about 30 minutes. Put the ice cubes in a tall glass, and add the orange juice and tea. Stir in the mint leaves.

A ROYAL AFFAIR

Theme: We need to be willing to serve each other in our marriage. If you treat her like a queen, she will make you feel like a king!

Verses to share and meditate on:

Matthew 20:26b-28, *Whoever wants to become great among you must be your servant, and whoever wants to be first must be your slave—just as the Son of Man did not come to be served, but to serve, and to give his life as a ransom for many.*

Proverbs 22:4

Matthew 18:4

Matthew 23:12

John 13:5, 14

Romans 12:10

1 Corinthians 9:19

Galatians 5:13b

1 Peter 5:6

Tonight's affair will be in your own home. Start by planning to put the kids to bed early or have them stay the night at Grandma's house. Earlier in the day, make sure you have all the ingredients you will need to prepare your husband's favorite meal. Make your evening fit for royalty by using the good dishes and candles for golden light on the tables. Enjoy the experience of good food and God's goodness to you as husband and wife.

Husbands: First of all, make sure you notice all the little extras your wife has done to make this evening wonderful. Thank her most affectionately and then treat your queen to a warm bubble bath! Draw the water for her and have soft, romantic music playing. Light tons of candles all around the bath. Lay out a fresh towel with her favorite bottle of lotion. Pour her an ice cold drink in a long-stemmed glass and leave her to soak for an hour while *you do the dishes!*

Wife: After your relaxing bath, escort your husband to his favorite chair and put his feet up while you treat him like royalty. Give him a neck massage. Next, he gets a good back rub. Then massage his feet and back with lotion. Tell him how good he smells.

In our marriage, we have to be willing to put the needs of our spouse ahead of our needs. Christ was our example in that He came not to be served, but to serve. He is our King, and yet He washed the feet of His disciples. He humbled Himself as a man and became obedient to the cross. He was willing to die for us so by believing in Him, we could live.

In our marriage we have to be willing to humbly give of ourselves to please each other. And in doing that, we please God.

RECIPES:

DINNER FIT FOR A KING

CRUSTED SIRLOIN WITH PORTOBELLO MUSHROOMS

- ¼ cup prepared horseradish
- ¼ cup spicy mustard
- 3 Tbsp minced garlic
- 2 Tbsp cracked black pepper, plus more for seasoning
- ¼ cup olive oil, plus 2 Tbsp for searing
- ¼ cup bread crumbs
- 2 (6 oz) petite sirloin steaks
- Coarse sea salt
- 2 Tbsp butter, to sear

Portobellos:

- 4 Tbsp butter, divided
- 1 Tbsp chopped fresh thyme leaves
- 4 portobello caps, sliced
- 1 tsp salt
- 1 tsp cracked black pepper
- ¼ cup beef broth
- Splash of vinegar

Directions:

Preheat the oven to 400°F.

Whisk together horseradish, mustard, garlic, 2 Tbsp black pepper, and ¼ cup of olive oil in a small bowl. Stir in the bread crumbs and set aside. Season the steaks on both sides with coarse sea salt and black pepper. Brush the horseradish bread crumb mixture on one side of the sirloin steaks.

In a large sauté pan over medium-high heat, add 2 Tbsp of oil and 2 Tbsp of butter. Sear the steaks for 2 minutes, then turn over and cook for an additional 2 minutes. Remove the steaks to a quarter sheet tray with a rack. Drain the excess oil from the sauté pan. Put the steaks in the oven and cook until the breading browns, about 15 to 20 minutes. Remove from the oven and let rest.

Portobellos:

In the same pan in which the steaks were seared, add 2 Tbsp of the butter and the thyme. Turn the heat to high and add the portobello mushrooms. Add the salt and pepper and cook until the mushrooms are soft and slightly colored, about 3-4 minutes. Stir in the beef broth and a splash of vinegar. Reduce until the liquid just coats the mushrooms. Stir in the remaining 2 Tbsps of butter to give the mushrooms a creamier consistency. Arrange the steaks on serving plates and top with the mushrooms.

GOLDEN PARMESAN POTATOES

- 6 medium potatoes
- ¼ cup flour
- ¼ cup Parmesan cheese
- ¾ tsp salt
- Dash of pepper
- ½ stick margarine

Directions:

Peel and cut potatoes in quarters. Combine flour, cheese, salt, and pepper in plastic bag. Melt margarine in baking dish in oven at 375°F. Moisten potatoes in water. Shake in bag to coat. Place potatoes in one layer in melted margarine. Bake at 375°F for one hour, turning potatoes over after 30 minutes.

GREEN BEAN BUNDLES

- Fresh green beans
- Bacon, split lengthwise
- ⅓ cup brown sugar
- 2 cloves garlic, minced
- ½ cup butter

Directions:

Partially cook green beans in microwave. Put 6-8 green beans together with 1 strip of bacon. Tie bacon around to make a bundle. Place in a greased 8 x 11 inch baking dish. Repeat with as many bundles as desired. Mix sugar, garlic, and butter. Bring to a boil and pour over beans. Bake at 350°F for 30 minutes uncovered, then 20 minutes covered.

RICH AND GOLDEN APPLE DUMPLINGS

- 2 cups all-purpose flour
- 1 tsp salt
- 2 tsp baking powder
- ⅔ cup shortening
- ½ cup cold milk
- 6 medium tart apples, peeled and cored

Sauce:

- 1½ cups sugar
- 1½ cup water
- ¼ tsp cinnamon
- ¼ tsp nutmeg
- 8 drops red food coloring
- ½ cup butter, cubed

Directions:

In a large bowl, combine flour and salt; cut in shortening until crumbly. Gradually add cold milk, tossing with a fork until dough forms a ball.

Preheat oven to 350°F. Roll out dough in 18x12 rectangle. Cut into 6 squares. Place an apple on each square. Place 1 tsp butter and 1 tsp cinnamon-sugar in the center of each apple. Gently bring up corners of pastry to each center; pinch edges to seal. Place in a greased 9x13 baking dish.

In a large saucepan, combine sauce ingredients. Bring just to a boil, stirring until blended. Pour over apples. Sprinkle with sugar.

Bake 375°F for 35-45 minutes or until apples are tender and pastry is golden brown, basting occasionally with sauce. Serve warm with ice cream.

I CHOOSE YOU!

Theme: Making good choices in our lives and in our marriage. God made man and woman but designed them differently.

Verses to share and meditate on:

Deuteronomy 14:2, *For you are a people holy to the Lord your God. Out of all the peoples on the face of the earth, the Lord has chosen you to be his treasured possession.*

Deuteronomy 30:19

John 15:16

1 Peter 2:9

This date with your mate is a guy/girl thing. Toss a coin to see who gets to choose what you will eat and what movie or video you will watch. If the girl gets to choose, it may be a romantic love story and eating healthy baked chips, sub sandwiches, and carrot sticks. If it's a guy thing, it might be pizza and a big bowl of ice cream while watching an action-packed movie! It doesn't need to be expensive or involved. It could center on something you already have at home. It's just that one of you gets to choose!

Remember that no matter who gets to choose, you've already made a great choice . . . each other! You knew you were meant for each other. Tell your spouse you are glad to have been chosen from among all others!

It is only because of God's plan and His design for your lives that you are man and wife. By being different in design as two unique people, we complement each other as one in marriage. Think of ways you can choose to improve your relationship with your spouse. God designed man to be head over the home and to provide for the needs of his family. He is to love, honor, and cherish his wife. The woman is to be his helper and is to love, honor, and obey. Choosing to follow God's plan will make for a happy, satisfied marriage. Thank Him for the love and contentment He has blessed you with from the day you said, "I do . . . I choose you!"

RECIPES:

FRENCH DIP SANDWICHES

- 1 package au jus seasoning
- 1 beef rump roast or bottom round roast (4 pounds)
- ½ cup soy sauce
- 2 garlic cloves, minced
- ½ tsp pepper
- 1½ tsp beef base
- 4 cups water

Directions:

Place roast in a 5-qt. slow cooker. Combine the soy sauce, garlic, and seasoning packet, and pour over roast. Add water. Cover and cook on low for 8-9 hours or until meat is tender. Remove roast to a cutting board; cool slightly. Thinly slice meat.

Serve on buns and use the juice from the meat for dipping your sandwiches.

HOAGIE SANDWICHES

- 8 soft hoagie buns (6-7 inch), split
- 1 bottle creamy Italian salad dressing
- 8 slices (1¾ oz each) provolone or mozzarella cheese, each cut into 4 pieces
- 8 slices American cheese, cut into 4 pieces
- ½ lb thinly sliced salami or summer sausage
- 1 lb thinly sliced cooked turkey and ham
- Lettuce
- Tomato slices

Directions:
On bottom halves of buns, layer salami, turkey, and ham slices. On top halves of buns, add cheese slices. Place buns on a cookie sheet and bake in 375°F oven for 8-10 minutes or until thoroughly heated and cheese is melted and a little crunchy on the edges.

Top each sandwich with lettuce and tomatoes and Italian dressing.

LOVE NOTES

Theme: We can never tell our mates enough how much we love them. Love notes are a great way to say what we often take so for granted. "I love you!"

Verses to share or meditate on:

Song of Solomon 1:2, *Let him kiss me with the kisses of his mouth—for your love is more delightful than wine.*

Song of Solomon 2:4

Song of Solomon 7:12

Song of Solomon 8:6–7

John 15:12

1 Corinthians 16:14

1 Peter 4:8

1 John 4:19

Read Song of Solomon in the Bible. It is a book of love notes written from one lover to his beloved. It was probably King Solomon and the Shulamite girl he was going to marry. You don't have to read far to see he was crazy about her. They spared no words in describing their love for each other. Their love was romantic and affectionate. Their love was as unquenchable as fire and as strong as death.

God has written us a love letter. It is the Bible. In it He tells us how much He loves us. One love note is in John 3:16. Another in John 15:12. Take time to thank Him for His great love.

Today you are going to leave love notes for each other in unexpected places or at unexpected times. Sometime it is easier to write down your feelings than it is to say them. You are each going to write seven notes; no two notes can be alike. Here are some examples.

Around a Symphony™ candy bar, wrap your love note, stating that you hear music when you are together.

Hide a love note in your spouse's coat pocket.

Tape a love note to the steering wheel of the car, saying that their love drives you crazy.

Place a special love note on his or her pillow to be read only at the end of the day.

Buy a CD with love songs on it and write a note that says your love is like that song.

Leave a red rose with your version of "Roses are red . . . "

Put love notes in your love's shoes, breakfast cup, desk drawer, lunch box, tractor cab, etc. Just use your imagination!

At the end of the day, share what fun you had with your notes. Talk to each other about your goals, dreams, and even fears. Thank your spouse for being your best friend and for listening to you and being there for you.

RECIPES:

CHOCOLATE CHIP COOKIES

- 4 cups flour
- 1½ tsp baking soda

- 1½ tsp salt
- 3 eggs
- 1½ cups butter
- 1 large cup sugar
- 1 cup brown sugar
- 1½ Tbsp water
- 6 oz chocolate chips
- Nuts, optional

Directions:
Blend eggs, butter, sugars, and water. Mix flour, soda, and salt. Add to egg mixture with chocolate chips and nuts. Bake at 375°F for 10 minutes. *Makes 36 cookies.*

OATMEAL COOKIES

- 2 cups brown sugar
- 1 cup shortening
- 2 eggs, beaten
- 1 tsp vanilla
- 1½ cups flour
- ½ tsp salt
- 1 tsp baking powder
- 1 tsp baking soda
- 3 cups quick oatmeal
- Powdered sugar

Directions:
Cream sugar, shortening, eggs, and vanilla. Add remaining ingredients. Roll into balls and then roll in powdered sugar. Press down. Bake at 375°F for 8-10 minutes.

SCOTCHEROOS

- 1 cup sugar
- 1 cup light corn syrup
- 1 cup peanut butter
- 6 cups Rice Krispies™
- 1 cup chocolate chips
- 1 cup butterscotch chips

Directions:

Combine sugar and syrup. Microwave on high, stirring every 30-40 seconds, until sugar dissolves. Do not boil. Stir in peanut butter until smooth. Add cereal and stir until coated. Pat into 9x13 pan. Melt chips in microwave, watch closely, and stir every 10-15 seconds until melted. Do not overheat. Spread over top of bars. Let set before cutting. *Makes 24 bars.*

SNICKERDOODLES

- 1 cup margarine
- 1½ cups sugar
- 2 eggs
- 2¾ cups flour
- 2 tsp cream of tartar
- 1 tsp baking soda
- 1 tsp salt

Directions:

Mix margarine and sugar thoroughly. Add flour, cream of tartar, soda, and salt. Roll into balls the size of a walnut. Roll balls in mixture of 2 Tbsp sugar and 1 tsp cinnamon. Bake at 375°F for 8-10 minutes.

SOFT SUGAR COOKIES

- 2 eggs
- 1½ cups sugar
- 1 cup margarine
- 1 tsp vanilla
- 1 cup milk
- 4 cups flour
- 2 tsp cream of tartar
- 2 tsp baking soda

Directions:

Beat eggs 1 minute. Add sugar and shortening and beat one minute. Add vanilla and milk. Sift dry ingredients and combine. Drop by spoonfuls on a cookie sheet. Bake at 350°F for 10 minutes. When cool, ice with frosting. *Makes 72 cookies.*

Frosting:

- 6 Tbsp butter
- 2 tsp vanilla
- 4 Tbsp milk
- ⅛ tsp salt
- 3½ cups powdered sugar

Directions:

Beat together on high for one minute. Spread on cookies.

STARS IN YOUR EYES

Theme: The stars and the heavens remind us of how great and mighty our God is. He created all we see around us in the vast starry sky, and yet He cares about each of us, even star-gazing couples.

Verses to share and meditate on:

Psalm 8:3-4, *When I consider your heavens, the work of your fingers, moon and the stars, which you have set in place, what is mankind that you are mindful of them, human beings that you care for them?*

Psalm 14:2

Psalm 19:1

Psalm 33:6

Psalm 136:7-9

Psalm 147:4-5

Psalm 148:3-4

Isaiah 40:26

Ecclesiastes 5:2

Grab some blankets and go outside for an evening under the stars! Lie down close together on your blanket and gaze up at the awesome handiwork of stars, planets, and galaxies. Get lost in the great expanse of the Milky Way.

Sip on a tall glass of tea or lemonade. Feed each other grapes and strawberries and chocolate-covered candy stars. Take in the wonder of a God so amazing in creating this vast universe of the sun, moon, and stars, and then realize that He also created you. He cares about you and desires to be a part of your lives each day.

Talk together about God's heaven and what you think it will be like to be in heaven one day.

Pick out a group of stars and claim them as your own. Pretend they were put there just for the two of you. Then each time you find them in the sky, they will remind you of your love for each other and for God.

As you enjoy your dreamy summer night together, compliment each other on things that make you shining stars in each other's lives. Together, whisper a prayer to God, thanking Him for this vast starry host He has created for us to enjoy.

RECIPES:

MILKY WAY™ CHEESECAKE BARS RECIPE

- 1 cup graham cracker crumbs
- 5 Tbsp coconut oil (you can also use melted butter)
- 16 oz cream cheese, room temperature
- 1 egg
- ⅓ cup granulated sugar
- 2 tsp vanilla extract
- 1½ cups chopped Milky Way pieces
- ½ cup chocolate chips for the filling (I use dark chocolate chips)

- ¼ cup chocolate chips for the topping
- ¼ cup mini chocolate chips for the topping

Directions:

Preheat your oven to 350°F.

Mix together the coconut oil—or melted butter, depending on what you used—and graham cracker crumbs and pat down into an 8×8 baking dish. Bake at 350°F for 9 minutes and then allow to cool while you prepare the filling.

For the filling: Beat cream cheese, egg, sugar, and vanilla extract together until smooth and creamy; it should take you two or three minutes. Mix in the Milky Way pieces and chocolate chips and pour over your cooled crust. Top with additional chocolate chips and bake for 30-35 minutes, until the cheesecake is firm and the edges are golden brown.

Cool for about 30 minutes and then refrigerate for at least an hour before serving. Just cut into bars and enjoy!

MILKY WAY™ CARAMEL CHEESECAKE BROWNIES

Brownie Layer:

- 1 cup butter, melted
- 1 tsp vanilla
- 4 large eggs
- 2 cups sugar
- ¾ cup cocoa
- 1 cup flour
- ½ tsp baking powder
- ¼ tsp salt

Cheesecake Layer:

- 16 oz cream cheese, softened
- ⅔ cup sugar
- 1 tsp vanilla
- 2 eggs
- 2 cups chopped Milky Way Simply Caramel Bites (1 large bag)

Directions:

Preheat oven to 350°F. In a stand mixer or with a hand mixer, combine melted butter with sugar and vanilla. Add eggs one at a time, beating well after each one. Add the cocoa and mix well. Then add the flour, baking powder, and salt, and mix until just combined; do not over mix. Set aside one cup of the brownie batter and smooth the rest into a foil lined 9x13 baking dish.

Now for our next layer . . .

With your stand mixer or hand mixer (cleaned off), begin making your cheesecake layer by beating cream cheese and sugar until smooth. Add the vanilla and then the eggs one at a time, beating well after each one. Pour the cream cheese mixture on top of the brownie mixture and using a spatula, smooth it evenly over the brownie batter. Sprinkle the chopped Milky Way Simple Caramel slices evenly over cream cheese layer. They should be close together and pretty much covering the cream cheese layer.

Using the reserved cup of brownie batter, drop spoonfuls over the top of the candy bar layer, scattering around. Use your spatula or a butter knife to gently swirl the batters. This will combine the cream cheese layer and top brownies layer a bit, which cover the candies in batter. This does not need to be perfect.

Bake at 350 for 35 minutes. Allow to cool completely before cutting into squares (at least an hour).

Notes:

When brownies are done baking, let cool for about 30 minutes, and then lift them all out of the baking dish with the foil (by grabbing the sides of the foil). This helps to cool more quickly. You can also set the baking dish on a wire rack to cool faster. Be sure to refrigerate the brownies when you are done serving.

MILKY WAY™ COOKIE BITES

- Ready-made refrigerated cookie dough
- Bite-sized unwrapped Milky Way candy
- Mini-muffin pan

Directions:

Preheat oven to 350°F. Take about a tsp of cookie dough and press it in the mini-muffin pan. Gently press a bite-sized Milky Way on top. Place the pan in the oven for 12 minutes. Remove and let cool completely. Use a knife to loosen the edges of the cookies, and they should pop right out!

GET PHYSICAL

Theme: Try a new activity together. Get physical and stay fit by finding a fun activity or exercise you both enjoy.

Verses to share and meditate on:

Isaiah 40:31, *But those who hope in the Lord will renew their strength. They will soar on wings like eagles; they will run and not grow weary, they will walk and not be faint.*

Romans 12:1

1 Corinthians 6:19–20

1 Corinthians 9:27

1 Timothy 4:8

2 Thessalonians 2:17

There are so many fun active things you can do as a couple.

Call a horse stable or some friends who own horses and set up a time to go horseback riding. Some places give lessons that include learning how to groom and saddle the horses and also basic things you need to know about horses and riding. This is a great activity if you like animals and being outside on a farm.

Golfing is another physical activity that is good for couples. You can learn from a friend or purchase some lessons. You don't know what you will like until you try. If nothing else, you will get some sun, fresh air, and lots of walking together. Miniature golf might also be fun too and wouldn't require golf clubs or golf shoes.

Water activities are fun, physical, and refreshing. Find another couple who likes to water ski and see if they would be willing to teach you. It might be challenging, but the water and the sun combined with just doing something together will be worth it. Keep trying.

Gardening is great exercise. Find the ideal spot and start tilling and digging in the fresh soil. Take your gloves and shoes off and notice how the earth smells and how cool and good it feels on your hands and feet. It's all part of God's creation. Work together digging rows and planting seeds and then watch as God provides rain and sunshine to make them grow. Work together weeding and harvesting your produce. You may even want to freeze or can extra vegetables and fruits. Sometimes it's rewarding to give extra to friends and neighbors.

If you don't want or have space for a garden, but enjoy fresh produce, go to gardens where you can pay to pick fresh or spend the day together at a farmers' market.

Winter activities are great for couples. There are snow skiing areas, cross-country skiing, or just plain old snow sledding or tubing down the hill. Rent some equipment and have some fun. All are good exercise. Just putting on all the coats and gear is a job! Afterward, warm up with a cup of hot chocolate together.

Check out your local YMCA and learn how to play racquetball together. Most clubs offer lessons and provide equipment. There would also be other activities there that the two of you would enjoy.

Many couples like to go bowling. Find a bowling lane, rent shoes and bowling balls, and just have fun. You will probably enjoy laughing at each other if you haven't been bowling in a while. Oops! Another gutter ball!

How long has it been since you took your sweetheart roller skating? So what if there are more kids than adults? You can skate together, hold hands, and pull each other up! Most rinks rent skates for the evening.

Trying something new is fun and exciting! When we do it together, it keeps our marriage fun and exciting too.

RECIPES FOR SMOOTHIES:

HONEYDEW/KIWI SMOOTHIE

- 2 cups cubed honeydew
- 1 small Granny Smith apple, peeled, cored, and chopped
- 1 kiwifruit, peeled and chopped
- 2-3 Tbsp sugar
- 1 Tbsp lemon juice
- 1 cup ice cubes
- Honeydew and/or kiwifruit slices

Directions:

In a blender, combine honeydew, apple, kiwifruit, sugar, and lemon juice. Cover and blend until smooth. Then add ice cubes; cover and blend until cubes are crushed and mixture is slushy. Garnish with additional honeydew and/or kiwifruit slices, if desired.

PEANUT BUTTER/BANANA SMOOTHIE

- 10 oz skim milk or plain soy milk
- 1 Tbsp natural peanut butter
- 1 medium banana

Directions:

In a blender, combine all ingredients and mix until smooth. Use 6 ice cubes for a thicker consistency.

STRAWBERRY/BANANA/FLAX SMOOTHIE

- ½ medium banana
- ½ cup frozen unsweetened strawberries
- 1½ cups skim milk or light soy milk
- 2 Tbsp ground flaxseed

Directions:

Place ingredients in blender and mix until smooth.

GREEN SMOOTHIE

- ½ cups water
- 1 cup spinach
- 1 celery stalk
- 2 or 3 baby carrots
- ¼ apple
- ¼ pear
- ½ fresh or frozen banana, peeled
- ¼ cup frozen cranberries
- A few cilantro with stems (optional)
- A few parsley with stems (optional)

Directions:

Place water, spinach, celery, carrots, and any optional ingredients into blender and secure lid. Blend for 30 seconds or until smooth. Add apple, pear, banana, and cranberries to the container. Blend until smooth.

PEANUT BUTTER SMOOTHIE

- 1 cup almond milk
- 2 cups spinach
- 1 frozen banana
- ½ pear
- 2 Tbsp natural peanut butter
- 1½ Tbsp unsweetened cocoa
- 2 Tbsp plain greek yogurt

Directions:

Place ingredients in blender and mix until smooth.

A HONEY-DO DAY

Theme: Working together and getting some of those extra jobs done always has its rewards. It's about giving of yourself to help do jobs we can't handle on our own and meeting the needs of your spouse.

Verses to share and meditate on:

> Genesis 2:18, *The Lord God said, "It is not good for the man to be alone. I will make a helper suitable for him."*

2 Chronicles 15:7

Ecclesiastes 4:8–10

Galatians 6:9–10

Ephesians 4:28

Ephesians 5:28–31

Colossians 1:10

Set aside a day that, by working together, you can get things done! Each of you needs to think of a job that you really could use the help of your spouse. It's called a honey-do list! It could be that the husband needs help organizing his office or shop and could use the organizational skills of his "honey." The wife might need the strong muscles of her "honey" to move around the living room furniture.

Maybe it's a project of cleaning out the attic or the garage together. Maybe it's a day of doing yard work or gardening. Every job seems easier and goes faster if you have someone to talk to and share opinions with while you are working. Talk about future plans or ideas while you are busy on the job. Stop for lunch and grab a pizza or burgers and a soft drink.

Later after a long, hot shower, you can rub lotion on sore muscles. Put your feet up and relax! Reflect on how working together makes you spend time together and brings you closer together as a couple. Think about how spending time with God brings us closer to Him too. Read from His Word. Then each of you can make a list of things that your "honey" does that makes you feel special and loved.

Honey, when you do this _____ , it makes me feel _____ .

RECIPES:

HONEY WHOLE-WHEAT BREAD

- 3 cups whole-wheat flour, divided
- 4 to 4½ cups white flour
- ½ cup nonfat dry milk
- 1 Tbsp salt
- 2 packages yeast
- 3 cups water
- ½ cup honey
- 1 Tbsp oil

Directions:

Combine 2 cups whole-wheat flour, dry milk, salt, and yeast. Warm the water, honey, and oil. Pour over flour mixture and beat for 3 minutes. Stir in 1 cup whole-wheat flour and 4-4½ cups of white flour. Knead. Let rise. Shape into two loaves and place in greased bread pans. Let rise. Bake at 350°F 40-45 minutes.

SPINACH SALAD WITH HONEY DRESSING AND HONEYED PECANS

- 1 (6 oz) package baby spinach
- 1 cup quartered fresh strawberries
- ½ cup thinly sliced red onion
- ½ cup fresh blueberries
- 3-4 cooked bacon slices, crumbled
- ¼ cup crumbled blue cheese
- Honeyed pecans

Honey Dressing:

- ⅓ cup white balsamic vinegar
- 2 Tbsp honey
- 1 Tbsp Dijon mustard
- ½ tsp salt
- ½ tsp black pepper
- ⅔ cup extra virgin olive oil

Directions for dressing:

Whisk together vinegar, honey, Dijon mustard, salt, and pepper. Add olive oil in a slow, steady stream, whisking constantly until smooth.

Directions:

Toss together first 4 salad ingredients and ⅓ cup dressing. Sprinkle with bacon, cheese, and pecans. Serve with remaining dressing.

HONEYED PECANS

- ¼ cup honey
- 1 cup pecan halves
- 1 Tbsp sugar
- ¼ tsp kosher salt
- Pinch of ground red pepper

Directions:

Preheat oven to 325°F. Microwave honey in a bowl on high for 20 seconds. Stir in pecan halves. Coat a parchment-paper-lined jelly roll pan with cooking spray; spread pecans in a single layer on pan. Combine sugar, salt, and a pinch of ground red pepper; sprinkle over pecans. Bake 15 minutes or until toasted, stirring after 8 minutes. Cool completely; break into pieces.

HONEY BREAD PRETZEL

Dough:

- 1 package dry yeast
- ¼ warm water
- ½ cup milk, scalded
- ¼ cup sugar
- 1 tsp salt
- 2 Tbsp margarine
- 2¾ cup flour
- 1 egg

Directions:

Dissolve yeast in the warm water and set aside. Add sugar, salt, and margarine to milk. Stir 1 cup flour into milk mixture. Add yeast mixture. Stir, then add egg and beat hard. Stir in 1½ cup flour. Save the last ¼ cup flour to knead dough. Put dough in a large greased bowl and cover and let rise until doubled. Punch down and shape into a ball. Let rest 5 minutes.

Roll out a long rectangle about 6 inches wide and 18-20 inches long. Spread on 1 or 2 Tbsp margarine, 3 tsps sugar and ½ tsp cinnamon. Roll up long ways and pinch edges to seal.

Twist roll by turning in opposite directions and shape into a pretzel shape. Cover and let rise until double. Bake at 350°F for 25 to 30 minutes.

Honey Glaze for Pretzel:

- 2 Tbsp sugar
- ¼ cup honey
- 1 Tbsp margarine

Directions:

Bring to a boil and pour on bread while bread is hot. Sprinkle with slivered almonds.

AN EXTRA SPECIAL ANNIVERSARY

Theme: Keep the thrill of romance alive in your marriage. Remember to seek after their love as you did when you were trying to capture their attention and affection right up until the day you were married.

Verses to share and meditate on:

Psalm 77:11, *I will remember the deeds of the Lord; yes, I will remember your miracles of long ago.*

1 Chronicles 16:12

Psalm 20:7

Psalm 119:55

Proverbs 10:7

Song of Solomon 1:4

Start by planning what you would like to do for your special anniversary together. Surprises are usually good, but they can also be disappointing sometimes. By planning together, you can both look forward to what you have decided will be fun. Think about going to a place that was special to you when you were dating or first married. Where did you get engaged? Think about going back to the place you went on your honeymoon. Was there a special park or restaurant that you went to a lot when you were dating? Watch your wedding video or pull out the old love letter you sent to each other. It's such fun to look back and reminisce. It might surprise you what the other one remembers about certain events.

Plan an evening out for dinner or a day away. A whole weekend with just the two of you would be great. To make your anniversary extra special, plan ahead; for five days before the big day, start pursuing your mate. Make it exciting, fun, and intriguing. You worked hard at capturing their heart when you dating, giving them that much desired attention and affection. So you can do it again! The pursuit will take time and energy, and you will need to be creative, but it will be worth it.

For five days before your anniversary, surprise your spouse each day with a gift or a card with sweet words from your heart or, alternatively, plan five short quality-time activities to do together. If your spouse likes to be the recipient of special acts of service, as a surprise each day you can show your love by doing a chore your spouse hates to do. Maybe for five days you can give extra hugs, kisses, or a back or neck rub if that's what your spouse enjoys. It will stir up curiosity and excitement as your spouse looks forward to seeing what you have planned every day. It will make you both look especially forward to your anniversary date.

Here are some ideas to pick from:

Give a package of red-hot gum or hot tamales candy. Write on a card, "Our love is red hot!"

Give any kind of breath mints or gum. Write on the card, "You take my breath away!"

Give a peppermint patty or any kind of mints. Write on a card, "Our love was meant (mint) to be."

Give any kind of nuts or nutty bars. Write on the card, "I'm nuts about you."

Give a soft, cuddly stuffed bear. Write on the card, "You're my teddy bear," "I can't bear a minute without you," or "Let's snuggle!"

Give a soft, cuddly stuffed puppy and a package of chocolate kisses candy. Write on the card, "I love those warm, wet puppy dog kisses."

Give a box of chocolates or favorite candy. Write on the card, "You're the sweetest" or "I'm sweet on you." If you can find heart-shaped candy, write, "My heart beats only for you."

Give a candle and write on the card "You light up my life," "You make me feel warm all over," or "Our love burns brighter each year we are together."

Give lip gloss and write on a card, "Keep your lips soft and kissable just for me."

Give roses. Write on the card, "Our love is a beautiful arrangement" or "You are my rose of beauty."

Hold hands. Give your spouse a back or foot rub after work. Sit close together at dinner or on the couch. Give extra cuddles, hugs, and kisses for the five days . . . and don't stop.

Plan five days of a short but special time alone together. Meet for lunch or pack a picnic basket and go to a park. Go for a drive and talk without your cell phone. Get up early and take a walk.

Think of an act of service you can do for your sweetheart each day for five days. Prepare a favorite meal, wash the dishes, fill the car with fuel, buy groceries, or surprise them with a favorite drink.

Do these things in pursuit of the one you married. It will make your anniversary extra special.

RECIPE FOR LOVE

- 1 cup of Romance
- 1 pinch of Humor
- 2 spoonfuls of Joy
- 1 lb of Compatibility
- 3 Tbsp of Trust
- 1 cup of Respect
- ½ lb of Sharing
- 1 tsp of Tenderness
- ¾ cup of Patience

Celebrating Life with Your Children

SOME OF THE MOST PRECIOUS moments are the times you spend with your children. Take time to make memories and to teach them important truths from God's Word and from His handiwork of creation.

FOLLOW THE TRAIL

Theme: God wants to show us the right path to take in our lives. We need to follow Him.

Verses to share or meditate on:

Psalm 16:11, *You make known to me the path of life; you will fill me with joy in your presence, with eternal pleasures at your right hand.*

Psalm 23:3

Psalm 25:4

Psalm 27:11

Proverbs 4:18

Isaiah 40:3

Matthew 16:24

John 12:26

1 Peter 2:21

Plan a day to go hiking or biking on a trail as a family. Many parks have bike trails or hiking areas. You will need the right equipment for your excursion such as good hiking boots, backpacks, and water bottles. If you don't own your own equipment, borrow bikes and helmets from a friend or rent biking gear from a sports shop.

Load up your backpacks with trail mix, granola or energy bars, and bottles of water or sports drinks. Take time as a family to notice and talk about God's creation surrounding you. Enjoy the different trees, flowers, birds singing, and small animals hurrying about. Notice the clouds and colors of the sky. Take in the breeze on your face and the warm sun on your back. While on the trail, take turns being the leader and talk about the responsibilities needed to lead the way and what it means to be a good follower.

When you need to stop and rest for a while, talk about how God has a path or trail He wants to guide us on through life. We need to be willing to let Him take the lead. Sometimes we try to run ahead of God, but other times we fall way behind. We need to stay close at His side so He can direct our lives.

Just as we need the right equipment in hiking or biking, we also need the right equipment when following God. If we are hiking or biking, we need a good map to show us the way. We also need our helmet for protection, good tires or hiking boots, water of course to refresh us, and tools, such as a compass or cell phone, if we have trouble along the way.

When following God, we have the Bible as a map to guide us, lead us, and make us wise along the way. Sometimes the path gets hard and we get tired and weary. We have the tools of prayer, encouragement, and love so we can help and refresh each other. Most of all, let God do the leading, and enjoy the sights and sounds along the way. It will be worth it all at the end of the trail!

RECIPES:

GORP

- ½ oz whole shelled (unpeeled) almonds
- ¼ oz unsalted dry-roasted peanuts
- ¼ oz dried cranberries
- 1 Tbsp chopped, pitted dates
- 1½ tsp chocolate chips

Directions:
Mix together in a bowl and enjoy.

CHOCOLATE CHERRY ENERGY BARS

- 2½ cups unsweetened puffed wheat cereal
- ½ cup pecan halves, chopped medium-fine
- ¼ cup dried cherries or dried cranberries, coarsely chopped
- 2 Tbsp sesame seeds
- 1 Tbsp ground flax seed
- ½ cup honey
- ½ tsp vanilla extract
- ⅛ tsp salt
- ½ cup mini semi-sweet chocolate chips or finely chopped bittersweet chocolate

Directions:
Position a rack in lower third of oven; preheat to 300°F. Line an 8-inch square pan with parchment paper, letting it overhang on two opposite sides.

Toss cereal, pecans, cherries (or cranberries), sesame seeds, and ground flax seed in a large bowl.

Combine honey, vanilla and salt in a small saucepan. Warm over medium heat, stirring, until the honey is more fluid and the salt is dissolved. Pour the honey mixture over the dry ingredients and fold until everything is moistened and sticky. Let cool for 5 minutes. Fold in chips (or chopped chocolate) until evenly distributed. Scrape the mixture into the prepared pan and spread evenly with a fork. Using the back of the fork, press the mixture very firmly all over. (Alternatively, cover with parchment paper and press firmly all over.)

Bake until the top is golden brown, about 35 minutes. (If in doubt, take it out so the honey does not burn.) Run a knife along the unlined sides of the pan to detach the bars. Let cool in the pan on a wire rack to room temperature, about 1 hour. Use the ends of the parchment to lift the bars from the pan. Gently peel off the parchment. Use a heavy sharp knife to cut into 16 bars or squares.

TRAIL MIX FOR KIDS

- 2 cups low-sugar, whole-grain cereal
- 1 cup raisins
- 1 cup dried fruit, such as cranberries, apricots, apples, or papaya
- 1 cup nuts, such as walnuts, almonds, or pistachios
- 1 cup sunflower seeds or pumpkin seeds
- 1 cup dark chocolate chips

Directions:
Combine in a medium-size baggie.

BEEF JERKY

- 4-5 lb thinly sliced beef
- 4 Tbsp soy sauce

- 4 Tbsp Worcestershire sauce
- 1 Tbsp salsa
- ½ Tbsp ginger
- 2 cloves garlic or ¼ tsp garlic salt
- ¼ tsp black pepper
- ½ tsp salt

Directions:

Mix ingredients in bowl. Pour over meat and marinate 4-6 hours or overnight. Put in dehydrator and cook until dry.

ENERGY BARS

- 1 stick margarine
- 6 cups miniature marshmallows
- ½ cup peanut butter
- 2 cups quick oatmeal or old-fashioned rolled oats
- 2½ cups Rice Krispies™
- 1½ cups raisins
- 1 cup peanuts

Directions:

Mix oatmeal, cereal, raisins, and peanuts. Melt margarine and marshmallows. Stir in peanut butter. Pour over dry ingredients. Spread in buttered 9x13 pan. Press firmly.

KIDS' CAMPOUT

Theme: Spending time with our family "in the wilderness" of the great outdoors while learning about how the people of God (called the Israelites) spent a lot of time in tents and ate manna.

Verses to share and meditate on:

Exodus 15:27, *Then they came to Elim, where there were twelve springs and seventy palm trees, and they camped there near the water.*

Genesis 32:2

Exodus 14:19

Exodus 16:11–15

Job 24:5b

Isaiah 41:19–20

Load up the tent, sleeping bags, pillows, PJs, flashlights, and food, and head off to a camping area or park. If you don't want to go too far from home, maybe you can rough it in your back yard.

Start by having everyone pitch in to help set up the tent. Unroll sleeping bags and find a spot for each one. Then round up firewood, twigs, and leaves to start a campfire.

Plan a scavenger hunt of treasures in the great outdoors. Search for a pinecone, maple leaf, smooth rock, dandelion, ladybug, earthworm, flower, feather, etc.

Play a game of flashlight tag. Flashlights are the only equipment needed, although you may need extra batteries. You'll need a large area that's not too hazardous to negotiate in the dark. One player is designated "it" and given a flashlight. "It" counts to 50 while the other players hide. When "it" finds someone, he or she shines the flashlight on the other player. That player then becomes "it," and the first player is free to go hide.

One of the best parts of camping is eating the food you cook over an open fire. Cut supple tree branches and whittle the ends clean with a sharp knife. Roast hotdogs on your sticks. Open a can of pork and beans. Eat them cold or place the can in the hot coals for warm beans. Munch on chips and carrot sticks. For a fun dessert, teach the kids how to roast the perfect marshmallow and then make s'mores with graham crackers and chocolate bars.

After dark, have everyone sit around the campfire and tell funny stories and sings songs the kids all enjoy. Sing silly songs and also praise songs to God for how great a God He is.

Find a good stop away from any lights and star gaze. It is amazing to think that those stars are the very same ones the Israelite people looked at when they were sleeping in tents in the wilderness. Talk about how they relied on God alone for their food and how He supplied manna, a bread-like wafer, for them every morning and night. Explain how they weren't supposed to save any for the next day, except for the day before the Sabbath when they gathered twice as much. On the Sabbath, they were not to gather or work. Talk about what that would be like! We can't imagine eating the same thing day after day, but that was God's way of supplying their food.

If you can't camp outside, camp inside your house! Make a tent in the living room out of blankets and roll out the sleeping bags. Turn the lights off and the flashlights on. Cook hotdogs and s'mores in the microwave or fireplace and eat picnic-style on a blanket spread out on the floor. It will still be a fun night as long as it is spent together!

RECIPES:

PAPER BAG EGGS

- 2 strips of bacon per serving
- 1 egg per serving desired
- Salt & pepper, hot sauce, ketchup
- 1 paper lunch bag per serving
- 1 green, pointy stick per serving

Directions:

Cut both bacon strips in half, giving you 4 pieces. Line the bottom of the paper lunch bag with the bacon to make a nice bacon nest for the egg.

Crack an egg into the nest.

Fold the top of the paper bag down carefully 2 times and poke a hole through the thick part with the stick. (Use a knife or scissors to make the hole first.)

Carefully hold the bag over the fire so the bacon cooks slowly and the fat melts. This makes an oily paper and bacon "skillet" for the egg. Take care and keep cooking it until the egg is done.

Eat it out of the bag . . . but put it on a plate! If you put it on your knee, the grease from the bacon will ruin your pants.

Use salt, pepper, and ketchup to your taste.

LUMBERJACK BREAKFAST PACKETS

- Sausages or Canadian bacon
- Frozen hash browns, or leftover cooked potatoes, diced
- Eggs
- Chopped tomatoes
- Green onions, if you like
- Shredded cheese

Directions:

Kids love to help make their own breakfast packets! Lay sausages or Canadian bacon on a double layer of foil that has been sprayed lightly with cooking spray. It is best to have the meat on the bottom so it can receive direct heat from the grill to cook properly.

On top of the meat, add a handful of frozen hash browns or diced leftover potatoes, an egg or two, and diced tomato and green onion if you like. Salt and pepper to taste.

Wrap up packet and place on a hot grill or in hot campfire coals for 15-20 minutes or until meat is thoroughly cooked.

Open it up and add shredded cheese and put it back on the grill with the cover down to melt the cheese.

CAMPFIRE BLUEBERRY ORANGE MUFFINS

- Blueberry muffin mix (also include ingredients to be added to the mix, as listed on box or bag)
- Oranges (as many as the number of muffins you plan to make)

Directions:

Stir up a box of blueberry muffin mix according to the package directions.

Cut an orange in half and scoop out all the orange flesh. Save orange flesh for another time, or strain and drink the orange juice.

Fill one half of emptied orange peel with blueberry muffin mix.

Cover the filled orange half with the empty orange half and then wrap in three layers of aluminum foil. Then just toss them in the fire. The orange peel will insulate the muffin mix from burning. The orange peel itself might blacken a little, but the mix in the middle will turn out steamed and delicious.

Keep turning the aluminum balls over and over in the fire, every minute or so. It usually takes about 10 minutes, but go ahead and pull them out and check them once in a while until they are firm in the middle.

Unwrap and eat with a spoon.

SPIDER DOGS

- Hot dogs (as many as you need to feed your family)

Directions:

You'll need a knife and some roasting forks or sticks. Cut the ends of each hot dog into quarters, leaving about 2 inches in the middle uncut. You want to leave enough uncut to stick the fork in. Roast the dogs over the fire or hot coals in a grill. The "legs" will curl out as the hot dogs cook. You can also do them in the kitchen at home over a hot stove burner.

PIE IRON PIZZA

- Bread
- Mozzarella cheese
- Pizza sauce
- Butter

Directions:

Making these is sort of like making a grilled cheese sandwich. First you butter two pieces of toast and put the buttered sides down onto the pie iron. Then you put pizza sauce and mozzarella cheese on the top of one slice of bread. Close the pie iron and cook over the fire.

BROWN BEARS

- 3 Tbsp cup ground cinnamon
- ⅔ cup white sugar
- ⅓ cup butter, melted
- 1 can refrigerated plain biscuit dough

Directions:

Combine cinnamon and sugar together in a bowl thoroughly.

Melt butter in another bowl.

Separate biscuits.

Form each piece of dough into a rope 4-5 inches long, making sure not to stretch them out too long. Wrap the dough pieces around proper campfire sticks. We find that patting the dough around the end of the stick to make a "cap" helps the dough stay on.

Hold the sticks over your campfire and slowly turn until the biscuit dough is browned and firm, which takes about 8-10 minutes. You can either remove the dough or keep it on the stick when you dip the cooked biscuits into melted butter and then into cinnamon-sugar.

HOT NUTELLA™ DRINK

- 4 cups milk
- ½ to 1 cup Nutella spread
- Bag marshmallows

Directions:

In sauce pan or microwave, heat milk until steamy. Add Nutella spread and stir to dissolve. Pour into cups and top with marshmallows. *Serves 4.*

TIME TO MAKE MEMORIES

Theme: Make a memory by spending time together doing a special activity each month. Teach your children that time together as a family is important to you. It may become a family tradition that gets passed on to the next generation.

Verses to share and meditate on:

Psalm 25:4–5, *Show me your ways, Lord, teach me your paths. Guide me in your truth and teach me, for you are God my Savior, and my hope is in you all day long.*

Deuteronomy 4:9

Psalm 27:11

Psalm 31:15

Psalm 34:1

Psalm 62:8

Psalm 119:12

Proverbs 17:17

Ecclesiastes 3:1

Colossians 1:28

Each month, plan a fun family activity. Make sure to use this time to teach your children things about God.

January: If you live where there is snow, have a snow day. Build a snowman, go sledding or ice-skating, or make snow angels. If you have never made snow ice cream with your kids, you have got to try it. Find 3 cups of loose, clean snow. Add 2 Tbsp milk, ¼ cup sugar, and 1 tsp vanilla. Stir and enjoy.

February: Spend an afternoon or evening making valentines. They could be for everyone in the family, or you could send the valentines to older people you know who might not otherwise receive a card. Make sure you have plenty of red, pink, and white paper. Use glitter, ribbon, doilies, lace, and different colored markers. It's fun to be creative! Let someone know you care and that they are special to God and to you.

March: Try making homemade play dough. Everyone loves the feel of clay in their hands. Shape and mold all kinds of things. Talk about how God is the potter and His people are the clay. He molds and shapes us so He can use us for His purposes. This is a recipe for homemade play dough.

1 cup flour, ½ cup salt, 2 tsp cream of tartar, 1 Tbsp oil, 1 cup water. Cook on medium heat, stirring constantly, until mixture is thick and becomes a ball all at once. Tint with food coloring and store in an airtight container.

April: Think about spring and the promise of new life. Color Easter eggs together and decorate them with all the fun colors of spring. Let your kids fill plastic eggs with candy and have them hide the eggs for Mom and Dad to find.

If you are able to have a hunt outside, look for signs of spring on the trees and in the flowers that are starting to come up. Talk about how we can have new life in Christ by trusting in Him for our eternal life.

Another idea for spring and new life would be to visit a farm with new baby animals or take a trip to a zoo or pet shop to admire all the different animals God has created.

May: May baskets are a fun thing to do on May 1st. It is called May Day, and typically you fill a basket or container with goodies and take it to a friend or neighbor. Set your May basket on the step, knock or ring the bell, and run away before they answer the door. (If they chase after you and catch you, they are to give you a kiss.)

May baskets can be made in different ways. You can design your own out of construction paper, or plastic cups with pipe cleaner handles work well. Fill them with popcorn, gum, and candy. Add flowers or spring designs to the outside. This can be a time to demonstrate that it is more blessed to give than to receive. This would be a good project to make and take to people in nursing homes or hospitals.

June: Father's Day is in this month, so how about making sure Dad is treated like a king? Since Father's Day is always on a Sunday, plan to make his breakfast with the kids cooking on Saturday so they won't be rushed. Let them do as much of the preparing as they can. All kids love to crack open eggs or flip the pancake. Watch them smile as they carry Dad's breakfast to the table and set it down in front of him. Go around the table and have each person tell one thing about their father that they are thankful for, and then be sure to remember to thank God for giving them a great Dad. (This idea is great for Mother's Day too when you treat her like a queen!)

July: Celebrate the Fourth of July holiday by making a birthday cake for America. Set aside a day to help the kids in the kitchen as they stir up a cake, bake it in the oven, and then frost and decorate it. Talk beforehand about ideas they have on what they want it to look like so you can have those decorating supplies on hand. As you work, take this time together to reflect on freedom and what it means in our country. Make sure to talk about true freedom, which only is found in Christ. He gave His life for us on the cross so we could be free from sin by trusting Him alone for our salvation.

August: This month in late summer seems to be a laid back month. Enjoy times doing laid back or lazy things. Go to the beach and relax in the sun. Build sandcastles with your kids. Late in the summer evenings, catch fireflies together and keep them in a jar. How about cranking a freezer of homemade ice cream by hand? Let each child have a turn cranking. It will be worth the hard work put into it as you enjoy each cold, refreshing spoonful. Each day God gives us so many good things, and we can reflect on those good things at then end of the day. They are called blessings!

September: Apples are just starting to be ripe for picking. Plan a day to visit an apple orchard and pick apples as a family. There is nothing tastier than a crisp apple fresh off the tree. Some places let you watch how apple cider is made and then give you a taste of it. When you are home, let the children help bake a pie or apple crisp or even applesauce from the apples you picked together.

October: Fall is a great time for picking pumpkins. Visit a pumpkin patch and let each child pick his or her own pumpkin. You can carve them together or paint faces on them. You may want to roast the seeds and eat them. If you have your own pumpkin patch, have each child write their name on a pumpkin when it is about the size of a baseball. Use a ballpoint pen and make sure it cuts through the skin of the pumpkin. As it grows, it will scar over in white, and the name will get bigger as the pumpkin gets bigger.

November: Get together as a family and choose a person who is shut-in or has no family close and make them a care basket. Go shopping together and find things such as hand cream, candy, cookies, small package of tissues, nail clippers, a small plant, books or magazines, or other things such as these. Deliver your basket as a family and spend some time with the person you have chosen and make a memory with them.

December: This is the month to bring out that favorite cookie or candy recipe and get everyone involved. Make it a yearly tradition the kids will remember and pass down to their children. Decorate sugar cookies with all sorts of sprinkles and fun candies. Make gingerbread men or a gingerbread house. Decorate with white frosting and all kinds of candy. Don't let it be stressful. You can buy the dough or a kit. Be sure you have lots of candy to decorate with and also some to eat!

RECIPES:

KICK THE CAN ICE CREAM
- 1 cup whipping cream
- 1 cup milk
- 1 beaten egg
- ½ cup sugar
- 1 tsp vanilla

Directions:

You will need a 1-lb. empty, clean coffee can and a 3-lb. empty, clean coffee can. In the small coffee can, combine all ingredients. Cover can and seal with duct tape; put it into the large coffee can. Layer ice and rock salt around the small can. When filled, cover large can.

Roll the can back and forth for 10 minutes. Open outer can; empty ice and water. Lift out the small can, wipe clean, and open. Scrape the sides and stir the ice cream. Replace cover and reassemble the cans with fresh ice and salt. Roll 5 more minutes. Open and enjoy!

CARAMEL SAUCE

- 4½ cups brown sugar
- 2 cups white syrup
- 2 (15 oz) cans sweetened condensed milk
- 2 cups butter or margarine
- 2 tsp vanilla
- Dash of salt

Directions:

Melt butter in a heavy saucepan. Add sugar, salt, syrup, and corn syrup. Mix well. Gradually add milk, stirring constantly. Bring to a slow boil. Cook until about 245°F or until firm boil stage, which is usually about 12-15 minutes. Remove from heat. Stir in vanilla. Serve with apple slices or make caramel apples on a stick.

ROASTED PUMPKIN SEEDS

- Pumpkin
- Salt and choice of spices

Preheat the oven to 300°F.

Using a spoon, scrape the pulp and seeds out of your pumpkin into a bowl. Separate the seeds from the stringy pulp, rinse the seeds in a colander under cold water, then shake dry. Don't blot with paper towels; the seeds will stick.

Spread the seeds in a single layer on an oiled baking sheet and roast 30 minutes to dry them out. Add spices: Toss the seeds with olive oil, salt and your choice of spices (see below). Return to the oven and bake until crisp and golden, about 20 more minutes.

Sweet: Toss with cinnamon and sugar.

Spanish: Toss with smoked paprika; mix with slivered almonds after roasting.

Italian: Toss with grated parmesan and dried oregano.

Barbecue: Toss with brown sugar, chipotle chile powder, and ground cumin.

4TH OF JULY KABOBS

- 9x13 pan of brownies (chilled and cut into 1-inch cubes)
- 1 pint blueberries, washed
- 1 pint strawberries, washed and hulled
- Large marshmallows
- Hot Fudge Sauce for drizzling, if desired
- Bamboo/wooden skewers

Directions:

Alternate threading brownies, fruit, and marshmallows onto wooden skewers. Drizzle with hot fudge sauce, if desired. Refrigerate until ready to serve.

GINGERBREAD HOUSES
MADE WITH GRAHAM CRACKERS

- 3 egg whites
- 1 lb powdered sugar
- ½ tsp cream of tartar
- 1 large box graham crackers
- Christmas candies for decoration

Directions:

Combine the egg whites and cream of tartar in a large bowl to make royal icing. Add powdered sugar 2 Tbsp at a time and blend the mixture with a mixer about 7-10 minutes on high speed or until the icing has the consistency of stiff peanut butter. Keep covered with a damp cloth. The icing will secure the graham cracker walls of the house and stick the candy decorations to the surface.

Place large spoonfuls of the royal icing into quart-size zip-style freezer bags. Avoid regular thickness sandwich bags because the plastic is too thin and will not hold up to the punishment of being used as a pastry tube. Approximately 1 cup of icing in each bag is enough. Make sure that each gingerbread artist has his or her own bag of icing. Seal the bags. Use scissors to snip ¼" off one corner of the icing filled bag. You now have an "icing tube." As you decorate, you'll squeeze the icing toward the snipped corner and use it to dispense icing on your gingerbread house.

Count out four whole, uncracked, unseparated, unbroken crackers. Break or saw 2 crackers in half to form the roof and the two sides of your house. Cut the two remaining cracker sheets to form end gable pieces. Use a gentle "sawing" motion with a serrated knife. Squeeze icing along the edges of a gable end and 1 whole graham cracker. Stick the side edge of the gable end cracker to the icing on the flat side of the wall cracker. The walls should hold each other up. Use plenty of frosting! Add the other gable end and wall in the same manner. Also, use a row of icing where the two walls will join at the corners. Add the roof crackers in the same manner as the wall crackers. Allow the icing to set for 15-20 minutes before handling the house again. Use your imagination and decorate the entire house whatever way you like.

HOW TO MAKE A MAY BASKET

The Basket

Mix one part glue with two parts water in a disposable cup.

Tear up strips of tissue paper into an assortment of shapes and sizes. Use an array of colors.

Dip the pieces of tissue paper into the glue mixture. Use your fingers to wipe away excess glue and paste the tissue paper to the clear plastic cup. Cover the entire outside of the cup. Make sure the pieces of tissue paper overlap. You can either place the pieces randomly for an abstract look, or you can place them in a pattern.

Allow the glue to dry thoroughly by leaving the cup to air dry overnight.

Use a paper punch to place a hole on each side of the cup. The holes should be parallel and about ⅛ inch below the lip of the cup.

Use piper cleaners to make a handle for your basket by feeding the ends into the holes and wrapping them around.

The Flowers

Cut or tear tissue paper into 4-inch squares. You can use multiple colors or one single color.

Place five squares on top of one another.

Pinch the squares in the middle and tie a piece of string around them.

Pull the pieces outward to fluff them into a flower shape.

Feed the end of a green pipe cleaner through the tied piece of string. Wrap the pipe cleaner around twice to secure it. Place the flower in the basket. If needed, cut the pipe cleaner down to shorten the stems. Repeat this flower-making process to fill the basket. Fill in the empty space around the flowers with crumpled green or brown tissue paper.

You can also fill the May basket with candy.

PIZZA AND GAME PARTY

Theme: In life we have to play by the rules, and the Bible is our rulebook. We need to learn to cooperate, play fair, and be honest.

Verses to share and meditate on:

Colossians 3:9–10, *Do not lie to each other, since you have taken off your old self with its practices and have put on the new self, which is being renewed in knowledge in the image of its Creator.*

Deuteronomy 25:15–16

Proverbs 3:27

Philippians 3:16

1 Thessalonians 4:6–7

2 Timothy 2:5

Spend a night together having pizza, games, and fun! You can make a homemade pizza together with everyone's favorite toppings, bake some frozen pizza, or order pizza delivered and ready to enjoy. Be sure to have everyone's favorite soda on hand too.

Fun Games:

1. Uno
2. Sorry
3. Candyland

4. Hi-Ho Cherrio
5. Twister
6. Aggravation
7. Dominoes
8. Checkers
9. Old Maid
10. Go Fish

When explaining the rules of each game, talk about how important rules are for us in anything we do. God gave us rules for a reason. He gave us the law so we could more easily see that we are sinners. Without rules, everyone plays how they think is right, and it just doesn't work. Only following God's way will free us from our sin and make us happy in life.

After game time, make some yummy treats together.

RECIPES:

EASY DONUTS

- A can of refrigerated biscuit dough
- Cinnamon-sugar

Directions:

Open a can of refrigerator biscuits. Poke a big hole in the center of each one with your fingers. Fry biscuits in hot oil until light brown on one side. Flip over and brown on the other side. Drain on a rack or on paper towels. Toss in a cinnamon and sugar mixture and enjoy while still warm.

BUBBLE PIZZA

- 1½ pounds ground beef, browned and drained
- 16 oz pizza sauce

- 2 cans buttermilk biscuits
- 2 cups shredded mozzarella cheese
- 2 cups shredded Cheddar cheese

Directions:

Preheat oven to 350°F. Stir pizza sauce and ground beef together. Cut biscuits into fourths or smaller. Fold into ground beef mixture. Add 1 cup mozzarella cheese and 1 cup cheddar cheese. Pour into greased 9x13 pan. Bake for 20 minutes. Put remaining cheese on top and bake 10 minutes longer. Let stand 10 minutes and serve. You may also use other meats of your choice and add other favorite pizza toppings that you like. *Makes 12 servings.*

STROMBOLI

- 1 package frozen bread dough
- Choice of meats: Canadian bacon, pepperoni, browned ground beef
- Sauerkraut
- 1 (16 oz) package of 4-cheese blend
- Parmesan cheese
- 1 can pizza sauce

Directions:

Thaw bread dough. Roll out to about 8x18 inches. Spread half the cheese down the middle. Spread the meat. Add the rest of the cheese on top of the meat. Roll up sides and pinch together. Twist into pretzel shape. Bake about 30 minutes at 350°F. Brush with butter and sprinkle with parmesan cheese and bake another 10-15 minutes. Slice in triangles and dip in warmed pizza sauce.

Hint: You may also add well-drained sauerkraut for Bavarian style. *Makes 10 servings.*

FAMILY DVD FUN

Theme: Learning what it means to be a family and the importance of family time together. Learning what it means to be a part of God's family.

Verses to share and meditate on:

Deuteronomy 4:9–10, *Only be careful, and watch yourselves closely so that you do not forget the things your eyes have seen or let them fade from your heart as long as you live. Teach them to your children and to their children after them. Remember the day you stood before the Lord your God at Horeb, when he said to me, "Assemble the people before me to hear my words so that they may learn to revere me as long as they live in the land and may teach them to their children."*

Deuteronomy 5:16

Psalm 22:27

Psalm 107:41

Proverbs 22:6

Luke 18:20

Colossians 3:20

Ephesians 3:14–15

Ephesians 6:1–4

Go together to a DVD store and let the kids pick out a good, wholesome movie to watch for the evening. If you children are old enough, you could let them make their own movie to watch. Let the kids run the camera and capture shots of what the family is doing throughout the day. Make sure it is on a day when you (Mom or Dad) are home, and you can help them with fun things to record.

Baking cookies together is fun, and you can enjoy them later when you are watching your movie! That evening you can all watch the movie together as you pass around the big bowls of hot buttered popcorn, cookies, and ice cold pop. It will be a great time of laughter and fun.

It can also be a time to reflect on being kind to one another. We are to obey our parents, and we are to love and forgive each other. Being part of a family means honoring and respecting each other. Thank God for each member of your family.

RECIPES:

PEANUT BUTTER COOKIES

- 1 cup shortening
- 1 cup peanut butter
- 1 cup sugar
- 1 cup brown sugar
- 2 eggs
- 2½ cups flour
- 4 tsp baking powder
- ¼ tsp salt
- 1 tsp vanilla

Directions:

Cream shortening, peanut butter, and sugars. Add eggs, dry ingredients, and vanilla. Shape into balls. Press with a fork and bake. Bake at 350°F for 10-12 minutes.

OATMEAL RAISIN COOKIES

- 1 cup margarine
- 1 cup brown sugar
- ½ cup sugar
- 2 eggs
- 1 tsp vanilla
- 1½ cups flour
- 1 tsp baking soda
- 1 tsp cinnamon
- ½ tsp salt
- 3 cups oatmeal
- 1 cup raisins

Directions:

Preheat oven to 350°F. Cream margarine and sugars. Add eggs, vanilla, baking soda, cinnamon, and salt. Cream together. Add flour, oatmeal, and raisins. Drop on cookie sheet. Bake for 10-12 minutes.

COWBOY COOKIES

- 1 cup shortening (2 sticks margarine)
- 1 cup brown sugar
- 1 cup white sugar
- 2 eggs
- 1 tsp vanilla

- 2 cups flour
- 2 cups oatmeal
- 1 tsp baking soda
- ½ tsp baking powder
- ½ tsp salt
- 6 oz butterscotch chips

Directions:

Preheat oven to 350°F. Cream together the shortening and sugars. Add the eggs and vanilla and beat well. Sift dry ingredients together and add to creamed mixture. Add butterscotch chips. Drop by spoonfuls onto greased cookie sheet. Bake for 10 minutes.

MACAROONS

- 2 cup sugar
- 2 cup white Karo™ syrup
- 1 cup peanut butter
- 2 cups corn flakes, crushed

Directions:

In a saucepan, bring sugar and syrup to boil. Remove from heat. Add peanut butter. Mix until smooth. Add corn flakes. Drop quickly by spoonfuls onto waxed paper. Cool.

PECAN CRISPIES

- ½ cup butter
- 6 Tbsp brown sugar
- 6 Tbsp sugar
- 1 egg
- ½ tsp vanilla

- 1¼ cups flour
- 1 tsp baking powder
- ¼ tsp baking soda
- ¼ tsp salt
- 1 cup chopped pecans

Directions:
Preheat oven to 375°F. Cream butter and sugars until light. Beat in egg and vanilla. Add dry ingredients. Stir in nuts. Add extra flour if it is too sticky. Drop by spoonfuls onto a baking sheet. Bake for 10 minutes.

MELTAWAYS

- ½ pound butter
- ⅓ cup powdered sugar
- ¾ cup cornstarch
- 1 cup flour

Frosting:

- 3 oz cream cheese
- 1 cup powdered sugar
- 1 tsp vanilla

Directions:
Preheat oven to 350°F. Mix butter, powdered sugar, cornstarch, and flour. Drop by spoonfuls on ungreased cookie sheet. Bake for 12 minutes. When cool, frost. Mix cream cheese, powdered sugar, and vanilla. Frost cookies. *Makes 4 dozen.*

LET'S HAVE A BALL!

Theme: When life is tough and the ball doesn't always bounce the direction we want it to, we need to trust God and ask Him to help us endure and stay in the game. Always give your best and don't give up.

Verses to share and meditate on:

Philippians 3:14, *I press on toward the goal to win the prize for which God has called me heavenward in Christ Jesus.*

Proverbs 4:23

Proverbs 16:17

1 Corinthians 9:12

1 Thessalonians 5:15

2 Timothy 2:10

James 1:4

Choose an activity to do together that includes the use of a ball. Bowling: Rent shoes, bowling balls, and lanes for the evening. Teach your children how to bowl and also how to keep score. Most bowling alleys have special lanes for children to use. You may have a lot of gutter balls, but you will also have a lot of laughter and fun.

Soccer: Find a soccer field that has goals already set up or set up boundaries and goals in your yard. Without a team you really can't play a game, but you can practice the fundamentals of the game and its rules. Teach the kids how to move and kick the ball around. The "goal" is just to have fun together!

Softball: Play catch and hit balls or have your own little softball game together. Use a big ball or T-ball if that is easier for the kids. Set up bases and teach them the rules of the game. Sometimes it isn't easy to hit the ball, but you just do your best and keep trying. Have a grand time just chasing them around the bases.

Croquet: Set up a croquet game in the back yard. Explain the goal and rules of the game and have fun hitting the balls through the hoops. The balls may not always go where they are supposed to, or someone's ball may knock out their ball. It's all part of the game, and it may show your children that things don't always go the way we want it to and how we should react when things don't go our way. Stay in the game and give it your best shot.

Our goal in life is to trust God in every situation. Sometimes life can be tough. We need to keep our eyes straight ahead and press on toward the goal or mark God has for us. He will make our paths straight when we look to Him. Play hard. Pray hard. Have a ball!

RECIPES:

M&M™ MONSTER COOKIES

- 12 eggs
- 2 lb brown sugar
- 4 cups sugar
- 3 tsp vanilla

- 3 tsp white corn syrup
- 8 tsp baking soda
- 1 lb margarine, softened
- 3 lb peanut butter
- 18 cups regular oatmeal
- 1 lb chocolate chips
- 1 lb M&M's
- 4 cups Rice Krispies™

Directions:
Preheat oven to 350°F. Mix all ingredients in a large bowl. Blending this with your hands is a good idea. Drop by ice cream scoopfuls onto ungreased jelly roll pan. These monsters can be made smaller! Bake for 12 minutes for large size and 10 minutes for smaller cookies.

Note: There is no flour in this recipe and it makes a large batch. Measurements in the list of ingredients are accurate!

WALKING TACOS

- 1 lb ground beef or turkey
- ½ cup diced onion
- 1 (1 oz) taco seasoning packet
- 6-8 snack-sized bags of Fritos™ or Doritos™

Suggested toppings:

- Black beans (warmed)
- Shredded lettuce
- Diced tomato
- Shredded cheese
- Sour cream

- Ranch dressing
- Salsa

Directions:

Brown ground beef or turkey and drain the fat. Add the onion to the meat and cook a couple of minutes until soft. Add the taco seasoning along with ½ cup of water and simmer until water is absorbed.

Crush your chips with your hands and open your bag. Add the meat mixture whatever toppings you desire and eat with a fork as you walk around! *Serves 6-8.*

POPCORN BALLS

- ¾ cup light corn syrup
- ¼ cup margarine
- 2 tsp cold water
- 2½ cups powdered sugar
- 1 cup marshmallows
- 5 quarts plain popped popcorn

Directions:

In a saucepan over medium heat, combine the corn syrup, margarine, cold water, powdered sugar, and marshmallows. Heat and stir until the mixture comes to a boil. Carefully combine the hot mixture with the popcorn, coating each popped kernel.

Grease hands with vegetable shortening and quickly shape the coated popcorn into balls before it cools. Wrap with plastic wrap and store at room temperature. *Makes 20 popcorn balls.*

GO FISH

Theme: God's Word tells us we are to be fishers of men. We all have friends and family who need to hear about Jesus Christ. We can be like a fisherman as we share about who Jesus is to us, wait patiently for the Holy Spirit to help them understand their need of a Savior, and then bring them in to know Him as their personal Lord and Savior.

Verses to share and meditate on:

Mark 1:17, *"Come, follow me," Jesus said, "and I will send you out to fish for people."*

Luke 5:10

Romans 1:16

2 Corinthians 6:2

Acts 22:15

2 Peter 3:9

Grab your fishing poles, tackle box, and lawn chairs. Go to a farm pond or lake near you and go fishing as a family. Pack a picnic lunch, a cooler of cold drinks, sunscreen, and bug repellent, and off you go!

You will need to purchase night crawlers for bait, or on the night before, have the kids go out with a flashlight and see if they can catch a few. You have to be quick! Another fun way to get night crawlers is to wet down a small area of lawn with the garden hose, squirt on lots of dish washing soap and then keep watering the area with the hose. The worms will slowly come to the top amidst the bubbles. You have to be patient.

After you arrive at your fishing spot and get everyone's lines in the water, sit back and soak up the sunshine. Have everyone listen to all the different nature sounds around the water's edge. There are usually frogs croaking and birds singing and leaves rustling in the trees. See who can come up with all the different sounds.

Besides catching fish, you can also try to skip rocks on the water, catch butterflies, pick wild flowers, or look for tadpoles. If you do find a tadpole, put him in a 5-gallon bucket of pond water. The kids will love to watch it grow legs and turn into a frog.

Hopefully you will catch some fish. Make sure you fry and eat the fish you catch and let the kids help you cook it. You can take it home and fry it, or cook it in a pan right over a campfire. The kids will think it is the best fish they have ever eaten since they got to catch and cook it!

If time permits, stay and watch the sun go down over the water. Catch fireflies together. As you sit around the campfire or dinner table, talk about how we can be fishermen like Peter and John were and about how patient a fisherman has to be when wanting to catch fish.

Peter and John and the disciples became fishers of men. That means they left their fishing nets and went out telling people about Jesus.

Talk to your kids about their friends who need to come to Jesus. It's a lot like catching fish. Most of all, it takes time and patience. Talk to your kids about what to say and how to say it. Witnessing is a lot like fishing.

You have to supply the bait. Share with them what Christ has done for you. Let them see Christ is real in your life. They will see something there they want and hopefully go after.

You put the hook in the water with bait on it; now you have to be patient. You can't make them grab onto what you are offering. Be patient and let the Holy Spirit convict them of their need for a Savior.

When the time is right, reel them in to Christ. Tell them what Jesus did for them on the cross. He died to take the punishment we deserve because we are all sinners. He offers us the free gift of eternal life. All we have to do is accept that gift and place our trust in Him alone to get us to heaven.

Come on . . . isn't this a great day to go fishing?

RECIPES:

TUNA SALAD SANDWICHES

- 2 cans chunk tuna, drained
- ¼ cup diced celery
- 2 Tbsp sweet pickle relish
- 2 hard-boiled eggs, chopped
- ½ cup Miracle Whip™

Directions:

Mix ingredients together in a small bowl and spread on sandwich bread.

CHICKEN SALAD SANDWICHES

- 3 cups diced cooked chicken
- 1 cup seedless grapes, halved
- ¾ cup diced celery
- ¾ cup pineapple tidbits, drained
- ½ cup chopped pecans (optional)
- 1 cup salad dressing

Directions:
Combine ingredients in a small bowl and use as a sandwich filling.

FROG-EYE SALAD

- ½ cup sugar
- 1 Tbsp flour
- 1 tsp salt
- 1 egg
- 1 cup pineapple juice
- 1⅓ tsps lemon juice
- 1½ quarts water
- 1½ tsps cooking oil
- 1 (8 oz) package Acini de Pepe (a pasta)
- ½ cup miniature marshmallows
- 2 (11 oz) cans Mandarin oranges, drained
- 1 (20 oz) can pineapple chunks, drained
- 1 (10 oz) can crushed pineapple, drained
- 1 (8 oz) carton whipped topping
- ½ cup coconut

Directions:

Combine sugar, flour, and 2 tsp salt in saucepan. Gradually stir in the egg and pineapple juice. Cook mixture over moderate heat, stirring until thick. Add lemon juice and cool to room temperature.

Bring the water, remaining salt, and oil to a boil. Add the Acini de Pepe and cook at a full boil until done. Drain and rinse. Rinse again and drain well. Cool to room temperature.

Combine egg mixture and Acini de Pepe by mixing lightly but thoroughly. Refrigerate overnight in air tight container. Add remaining ingredients and mix lightly. Chill in air tight container for up to a week, if necessary.

DIRT CUPS

- ½ cup butter or margarine, softened
- (8 oz) package cream cheese, softened
- 1 cup powdered sugar
- 3½ cups milk
- 2 (3.4 oz each) packages instant vanilla pudding and pie filling
- 1 (12 oz) container frozen whipped topping, thawed
- 1 pkg Oreo™ cookies, crushed
- 6-8 clear plastic cups
- Gummy worms

Directions:

Cream together butter or margarine, cream cheese, and powdered sugar. In another bowl, mix milk and dry pudding. Combine the two mixtures. Fold in whipped topping.

In the bottom of each cup, put a layer of crushed cookies. Add a layer of the filling mixture and another layer of the cookies. Add remaining filling and top with remaining cookies.

Refrigerate overnight. Before serving, poke gummy worms in the top.

Also pack carrots, grapes, apples, cheese slices, fish-shaped crackers, and shark bite fruit snacks. Enjoy!

WATER AND WAVES

Theme: We need to keep our eyes on Jesus and trust Him when the water and waves around us seem so big and our faith seems so small. God is always in control. He can calm the water and waves, and He can calm His children.

Verses to share or meditate on:

Psalm 37:3–5, *Trust in the Lord and do good; dwell in the land and enjoy safe pasture. Take delight in the Lord and he will give you the desires of your heart. Commit your way to the Lord; trust in him and he will do this.*

Psalm 40:4

Psalm 46:1–2

Matthew 14:25–31

Mark 11:22–23

Hebrews 11:1

Get ready for some water fun! Go to a local pool or water park and enjoy lots of swimming, sliding, and splashing. If you enjoy the feel of sand between your toes, grab your beach towels, buckets and shovels, and Frisbees, and head for the beach. Don't forget the camera! Spend time together building sandcastles or burying Dad under the sand.

Play catch in the water with beach balls or lounge on inner tubes and soak up some rays. Make sure to have life jackets or floaties for the kids who need them. Don't forget the sunscreen and sunglasses.

In the winter you can still enjoy water fun by going to a local YMCA, or you could treat the family to a motel and enjoy the pool and hot tub there. If it is possible for you, take advantage of the lower weekday rates.

Take time on your day of water fun to reflect on the Lord. He spent a lot of time on the water. He even walked on the water to get to the boat His disciples were in. Peter saw the Lord coming, and when the Lord told him to come and join Him, Peter stepped out of the boat, and he too was walking on the water to meet Jesus. That is, until he took his eyes off the Lord and started to look at the water and waves around him. Then he started to sink! Our troubles always begin when we take our eyes off the Lord. We need to focus on Him and trust what He is doing. We need to put our faith in Christ alone to help us as we face the waves and deep waters of life.

RECIPES:

FRESH SALSA

- 9 Roma tomatoes
- ½ chopped onion
- Garlic salt (to taste)
- 1 jalapeño pepper (optional)

Directions:

Chop tomatoes in food processor. Empty ingredients into another bowl. Chop onion with food processor. Add to first mixture. Cut pepper in half and remove seeds. By hand, cut jalapeño pepper into very small slices. Mix. Add garlic salt to taste. Serve with tortilla chips.

SUPER SIMPLE FISH TACOS
- 1 lb tilapia or cod filets
- 1½ Tbsp olive oil
- 1 Tbsp no salt all-purpose seasoning
- 1½ cups broccoli slaw
- 8 whole-wheat tortillas or white corn tortillas
- ½ cup plain yogurt or ranch dressing
- 1 cup loosely chopped cilantro
- 2 small limes, halved
- 1 sliced avocado (optional)

Directions:

Sprinkle seasoned salt on filets. Sauté fish in olive oil until fish flakes easily—about 8-10 minutes, flipping once. Remove from heat.

To assemble tacos, evenly distribute and layer ingredients on tortillas. Starting with fish, add broccoli slaw, yogurt or ranch dressing, cilantro, and avocado. Squeeze lime juice over all just before serving.

CHICKEN WRAPS
- 4 whole-wheat wraps (8 inches)
- 2 cups store-bought rotisserie chicken, shredded
- ½ cup shredded carrots
- 1 avocado, thinly sliced
- 1 cup baby spinach leaves
- ¼ cup of your favorite fat-free/low-fat dressing (about 1 Tbsp per wrap)

Directions:

Place wraps side by side on a flat surface. Divide chicken into four portions (about ½ cup each). Place a portion of chicken on each wrap. Top each wrap with carrots, avocado, and spinach. Drizzle dressing evenly over each wrap. Roll each wrap up tightly and cut on the diagonal. Serve immediately or wrap tightly in aluminum foil and refrigerate for lunch the next day.

WAVES OF MELONS

- ½ cantaloupe
- ½ honeydew melon
- ¼ watermelon
- 15 bamboo skewers

Directions:

Remove the seeds from each of the melons. Using a melon baller, scoop the flesh of each melon into balls. Place the balls in a large bowl. Cover and chill well.

To serve, skewer one ball of each type of melon onto a bamboo skewer. Repeat until all the fruit is used.

FRESH LEMONADE

- 6 cups water
- 1 cup plus 2 Tbsp sugar
- ½ cup freshly squeezed lemon juice

Directions:

Boil the water and add the sugar. Boil for 2 minutes and let cool. Add the lemon juice and ice. Serve with lemon slices.

LET'S ROLL

Theme: God is always there to guide us and give us strength. When we fall down, God picks us up and helps us get going again.

Verses to share and meditate on:

Psalm 46:1, *God is our refuge and strength, an ever-present help in trouble.*

Psalm 27:1

Psalm 29:11

Psalm 32:8

Psalm 37:23

Psalm 40:1–2

Proverbs 3:6

Proverbs 16:9

2 Corinthians 12:9

Philippians 4:13

Plan a time to go roller skating with your family. Find a rink in your area and if you don't have your own skates or inline skates, you can rent them. If it's nice outside, go skating together in a park or on a paved trail and enjoy the great outdoors. Skate next to your kids so you can help them and also so you can talk about things that are going on their lives. Kids want to talk about their friends and school, so be ready to listen.

Sometimes skating rinks will have different activities like limbo or "how low can you go." That's where you take turns skating under a horizontal pole and if you touch it, you are out. Another activity could be ladies' choice, where the girls get to ask someone to skate with them. Try skating backwards with a partner who is skating forward. It is hard to skate backwards so the individual doing that will have to rely on the partner to guide them and pick them up if they fall down. That's how it can be with God our Heavenly Father too. He is there to guide us when we can't seem to find our way or don't know what is ahead of us. He is always there to pick us up when we fall or stumble. He is our help and our strength. He goes along with us, and we know we can trust Him to lead us along the way.

RECIPES YOU CAN ROLL WITH!

OVERNIGHT CARAMEL ROLLS

- 3 cups warm water
- 1 package yeast
- 1 cup sugar
- 2½ tsp salt
- 1 stick melted margarine
- 2 eggs
- 8 cups flour

Directions:

Start dough at 4 or 5 in the afternoon. Mix yeast, sugar, salt, water, and eggs together. Add enough flour to make stiff. Do not knead. Make into rolls at 9 or 10 o'clock. Roll into rectangle shape. Brush with melted margarine. Cover with brown sugar and sprinkle with a lot of cinnamon. Put into 2-9x13 pans already filled with topping. Cover with damp towel overnight. Bake next morning at 375°F for 25-30 minutes.

Topping:

- ¾ cup margarine
- 1½ cups brown sugar
- 6 Tbsp white corn syrup
- 3 Tbsp water

Directions:
Heat together in sauce pan. Bring to boil. Pour into 9x13 pans. Sprinkle with pecans if you like nuts. *Makes 24 rolls.*

BEST CINNAMON ROLLS

- ½ cup margarine
- ½ cup sugar
- 2 tsp salt
- 1 cup cold water
- 2 eggs
- 8 cups flour
- 2 packages yeast
- ½ cup water

Directions:
Pour 1 cup boiling water over margarine, sugar, and salt. Add 1 cup cold water and eggs. Add yeast that has been dissolved in 2 cups warm water. Add 8 cups flour. Let rise. Roll out, sprinkle sugar and cinnamon mixture over dough. Roll up and slice. Makes enough for 2-9x13 pans.

Topping:

- 6 Tbsp margarine
- ½ cup brown sugar
- ½ cup white corn syrup

Directions:
Melt and stir for each 9x13 pan. Bake at 350°F for 25-30 minutes. *Makes 36 servings.*

QUICK ROLLS

- 1¾ cups very warm water
- ⅓ cup margarine
- ½ cup sugar
- 1 tsp salt
- 2 eggs, beaten
- 3 cups flour
- 2 packages yeast

Directions:
Put in bowl and blend: water, margarine, sugar, and salt. Add eggs. Mix together flour and yeast. Add liquid mixture to flour mixture. Beat 5 minutes with mixer. Add 3 more cups flour; mix well by hand. Put on floured surface and knead until elastic. Cover with plastic on surface and let set 20 minutes. Make into rolls (any shape or size) and place on buttered cookie sheet. Let rise 45-60 minutes. Bake at 375°F for 15-20 minutes (until light brown). Remove from oven and butter tops. *Makes 24 rolls.*

SNOW DAY

Theme: Enjoying God's beauty when He creates a fresh blanket of snow. God will make our hearts pure and whiter than new-fallen snow when we ask Him to forgive us for our sins.

Verses to share and meditate on:

Isaiah 1:18, *"Come now, let us settle the matter," says the Lord. "Though your sins are like scarlet, they shall be as white as snow; though they are red as crimson, they shall be like wool.*

Job 37:6

Psalm 51:7

Proverbs 25:13

Matthew 5:8

Philippians 4:8

1 John 1:9

What could be more fun than a day of playing in the snow? Put on your snow pants, heavy coat, scarf, and mittens. Bundle up because today is a day in the snow. There are so many fun things to do. Probably the number one thing is to build a snowman together. Building a fun fellow out of snow is hard work, so everyone needs to roll or pat. Then you need to decide what type snowman he will be and dress him accordingly. He may be a farmer snowman or a cowboy snowman. There are lots of different hats you could choose!

Sledding or tubing is tons of fun. Pile on the sled together and feel the wind and snow in your face as you race down the snow-covered hill. Maybe you could build a snow fort or tunnel through the snow. There is always a spot to make snow angels with your little angels. And if they are not feeling angelic, try making snow balls and having a snow ball fight or snowball throwing contest. Maybe you just want a more tranquil snow experience of catching snowflakes on your eyelashes and tongue. If you have fresh snow, try making snow ice cream. The kids will love it.

When you head back inside to get warm, there are still some fun activities you can do together on your snow day. Enjoy cups of hot chocolate together to get your hands and tummies warmed back up. Bake a batch of cookies with the kids or make edible snowmen using large marshmallows, chocolate chips for their eyes and mouth, and pretzel sticks for arms. Stack three marshmallows on top of each other and hold them together with frosting. Place a square of chocolate bar on the bottom. They may be too cute to eat!

Talk with your children about how God sends us the snow from His heavenly snow houses and how God give us the picture of our sins being made as white as snow when we confess them. Sometimes we do things that are wrong and not pleasing to God. He loves us and wants to make us pure and clean, just like the snow. All we need to do is ask for His forgiveness and accept the gift He offers us through trusting in His Son Jesus who died for us on the cross.

RECIPES:
Kids will have a lot of fun making these cold weather recipes!

SNOW ICE CREAM

- 1 gallon snow
- 1 cup white sugar
- 1 Tbsp vanilla extract
- 2 cups milk

Directions:

When it starts to snow, place a large, clean bowl outside to collect the flakes. Or carefully scoop up some fresh white snow! Stir in sugar and vanilla to taste, then stir in just enough milk for the desired consistency. Serve at once.

LEMONY SNOWBALLS

- ½ cup butter, soft
- ⅔ cup sugar
- 1 egg
- ¼ cup lemon juice
- 1¾ cup flour
- ¼ tsp salt
- ¼ tsp baking soda
- ¼ tsp cream of tartar
- Powdered sugar to use after snowballs have baked

Directions:

Cream butter and sugar together in mixing bowl. Add egg and lemon juice. Blend together. Add dry ingredients, salt, baking soda, cream of tartar, and flour. Stir together until well blended. Preheat oven to 350°F. Roll dough into small balls and place on cookie sheet. If dough is too sticky to handle, chill for 2 hours. Bake snowball cookies for 10-12 minutes until bottoms are lightly browned. Move to cooling rack or sheet of waxed paper. After cookies have cooled slightly so you can handle them, roll them in powdered sugar. *Makes about 24.*

SNOWBALL SURPRISES

- ¾ cup butter
- ½ cup sugar
- 1 egg
- ½ tsp vanilla
- ¼ tsp salt
- 1¾ cup flour
- Peanut M&M's™ or other chocolate candies
- Powdered sugar to use after snowballs have baked

Directions:

Preheat oven to 350°F. In mixing bowl, cream butter, sugar, and egg together. Stir in vanilla, salt, and flour to creamed mixture and mix until well blended. Roll dough into balls hiding a chocolate candy inside each ball. Place on cookie sheet and bake for 10-12 minutes until bottoms are lightly browned. Move to cooling rack or sheet of waxed paper and cool several minutes. Roll each cookie in powdered sugar and place on serving platter. Enjoy! *Makes about 30.*

BAKED ICE CREAM SNOWBALLS

- Broken cookies
- Ice cream
- 3 egg whites at room temperature
- ¼ tsp cream of tartar

- ¼ cup sugar
- ½ tsp vanilla

Directions:

In the bottom of six small oven-safe dishes, often called ramekins, place broken cookies. Add your favorite ice cream to the ramekins to fill the dish. Place the ramekins in the freezer while you finish preparing this fun, cold weather recipe.

Preheat oven to 400°F. In mixing bowl add the egg whites. With your mixer, whip egg whites several minutes until they look like soft peaks. Add the cream of tartar, sugar, and vanilla. Continue whipping in the mixer for several minutes until peaks become stiff.

Take the ice cream out of the freezer and add the egg white mixture (meringue) to the top of each ice cream dish. Completely cover the ice cream with the meringue. Place on cookie sheet and bake for 5-10 minutes until the meringue is browned. This won't take long to brown. Now you have your baked snowballs that you can decorate with chocolate syrup or eat as is.

TORTILLA SNOWFLAKES

- 1 package tortilla wraps
- Oil
- Powdered sugar

Directions:

Using kitchen scissors, have kids cut out tortilla snowflakes just like they would make snowflakes out of paper. Fry slightly in oil and sprinkle with powdered sugar.

SNOWBALL DESSERT

- 8 oz cream cheese, softened
- ½ cup butter, softened
- ¼ tsp vanilla extract
- ¾ cup powdered sugar
- ¾ cup cookie crumbs or miniature chocolate chips
- Powdered sugar for rolling

Directions:

In a mixing bowl combine cream cheese, butter, and vanilla. Cream together. Add in powdered sugar. Blend. Stir in cookie crumbs or mini chips. Shape into a ball. Lay out a sheet of plastic wrap and scatter powdered sugar over the top. Place dessert ball on top of sugar and roll around to coat entire ball. Wrap up in plastic wrap and chill several hours. Serve with graham crackers, plain vanilla cookies, or shortbread cookies.

POPCORN SNOWMAN

- 2½ quarts popped corn
- ¼ cup butter
- 1 (10 oz) package marshmallows
- 1 tsp vanilla

Directions:

Pop popcorn and set aside. In a saucepan over low heat, melt butter and marshmallows, stirring constantly until smooth. Stir in vanilla. Pour over popped popcorn and mix until well coated. With buttered hands, form into snowball shapes. Make one large ball for the bottom, one medium ball for the torso, and a smaller ball for the head. Use candy or nuts for eyes, nose, mouth, and buttons.

HOT CHOCOLATE MIX

- 3-4 cups powdered milk
- ½ cup cocoa
- ¾ cup coffee creamer
- 1 (3.4 oz) package instant vanilla pudding and pie filling
- 1 (3.4 oz) package chocolate pudding and pie filling
- ½ tsp salt
- 1 cup powdered sugar
- 1 cup sugar

Directions:

Stir ingredients until blended. Store in tight container. For a single serving, mix 2-4 Tbsp in 8 ounces of hot water.

IT'S MY BIRTHDAY!

Theme: Every child has one special day they can call their own. It's their birthday! God made them very unique and special and loves them very much. Let them know how special they are to you and how very much they are loved.

Verses to share and meditate on:

Psalm 139:13–16, *For you created my inmost being; you knit me together in my mother's womb. I praise you because I am fearfully and wonderfully made; your works are wonderful, I know that full well. My frame was not hidden from you when I was made in the secret place, when I was woven together in the depths of the earth. Your eyes saw my unformed body; all the days ordained for me were written in your book before one of them came to be.*

Exodus 19:5

Psalm 135:4

Ephesians 2:10

1 Peter 2:9

Plan to do something special for each child's birthday. It could be their favorite breakfast on their special day. It could be dinner with the family with cake and ice cream for dessert. Having a theme birthday party can be very exciting and fun! Party or paper-type stores will have paper plates, napkins, balloons, and all kinds of things you can add to your theme.

Make sure to include brothers, sisters, Grandmas, and Grandpas so they can all be in on the fun!

Younger Kids Party Ideas:

Circus and Clown Party: Purchase some face paint and make everyone look like a clown. Serve hot dogs and popcorn and soda. Let each child decorate their own clown cupcake. Place a sugar ice cream cone upside down on a frosted cupcake to be the clown's hat. Let them add candy to the cupcake for their clown's eyes and nose and mouth.

Cowboy or Cowgirl Party: Purchase red bandanas for the boys and pink for the girls. Help them tie them loosely around their necks like a cowboy. Buy or make sheriff badges for everyone to wear. Have them play "Pin the tail on a Horse." Make a horse or boot-shaped cake and serve with ice cream. Make sure the birthday boy or girl gets to wear a cowboy hat!

Princess Party: Purchase each girl a tiara crown to wear. Make sure the birthday girl has a fluffy boa to wear so she feels special. Have candy rings and candy necklaces for each one. Depending on the age, you might let them put on lipstick and make-up or get their nails done. Make princess placemats using markers and stickers to color and decorate with. Serve cupcakes with pink fluffy frosting sprinkled with edible glitter or pretty sprinkles.

Race Cars: Make signs to put around the room such as caution, pit stop, oil change, hot rod, etc. Also make flags out of checkered material, attach them to a dowel stick, and place them in a container in the middle of your table. Place toy cars on the table as a prize for everyone to take home. Let the kids rev up their engines and run relay races. Serve cake made in the shape of a car or in the shape of a big wheel. Have "turtle wax" sundaes with ice cream, hot fudge, and nuts.

Tea Party: Plan a pretty tea party with old purses, grown-up hats, and shoes to wear. Have each girl bring her favorite doll to the tea party as her guest. Use tea sets to serve juice and have fun snacks of crackers and cheese and a dessert of cookies and ice cream. Purchase string beads for each girl to wear and also take home.

Pirate's Treasure Chest: Make black eye patches out of felt and elastic. Purchase blue handkerchiefs to tie as a scarf on your little pirate's heads. Have a treasure hunt. Serve cake in the shape of a big treasure chest and have goodie bags with gold candy coins in them. You could also have the little mates cut swords out of heavy paper and then color or decorate them. Make a "Captain" name tag for the birthday child as a special treat.

Teddy Bear Picnic: Have each little girl bring her favorite teddy bear to the birthday party. Make it a real picnic by laying blankets on the ground outside on the grass. (Inside, of course, if the weather is bad.) Pack a picnic lunch of sandwiches, chips, fruit (such as straw"bear"ies), and drinks. If there is a sidewalk at hand, let the girls play hopscotch or tag while holding their teddy bears. Serve cupcakes with teddy bear shaped graham crackers on top.

Train Party: Many kids are fans of Thomas the Train. You can make railroad crossing signs to have at the front door. Then use masking tape to have railroad tracks on the floor. Give each child a red bandana and help them tie it loosely around their necks. If you can find wooden train whistles, the kids would love that and would have something fun to take home. Find an engineer's cap for the birthday child to wear because it is their special day! Make a train birthday cake with mini loaf pans for each car. Let the kids help decorate the train cars with some adults helping. Use Oreo™ cookies for wheels. You can also scoop out the train cars and fill them with edibles that look like sand (crushed graham crackers), logs (Kit Kat™ candy bars), coal (Cocoa Puffs™ cereal), etc. Make sure to do a lot of *chugga chugga choo-choos* all during the party. You could read the story of *The Little Red Caboose* or *The Little Engine That Could.*

Older Kids Party Ideas:

Hawaiian Luau: Get out the tiki torches and leis and be ready to do the limbo! See who can twirl a hula hoop the longest. Go bowling with coconuts as balls and pineapples as pins. Play musical beach towels by walking on towels as the music plays. The one who doesn't get to a towel is out. Serve Hawaiian punch and cake!

Bon Fire Birthday: Roasting hot dogs, marshmallows and creating s'mores will be part of the fun around the bonfire or fire pit. After it is dark, play "Capture the Flag" using glow sticks. You will need a large space to play in. Divide the space into two sides. Then divide the players into two teams and give each team a glow stick (this will be the flag) and every player a flashlight. Each team must hide their glow stick somewhere on their side of the playing space. At least an inch of the stick must be visible.

The object is to sneak onto the other team's side and steal their glow stick. If someone from the other team shines their flashlight on you and calls out your name, then get you must go to their prison cell. You can only get out if one of your team members "tags" you free with a flashlight; then both of you must make it back across to your side without being "tagged" by a flashlight again. The winner is the team that captures the other team's glow stick first and makes it back to their team's side.

Mexican Fiesta: Let the fun begin with Mexican style music and bright colors for decorating. Serve Mexican food such as tacos, burritos, chips and salsa and sodas to drink. Play musical sombrero. Pass the sombrero around and when the music stops, the person holding the sombrero is out. Last one standing is the winner. Have a nacho eating contest where the person standing behind feeds the person in front of them chips and nacho cheese. Have a "Battle of the Tacos." Put a hard shell taco over the handle of a wooden spoon. Each person tries to knock off the others' taco without hurting his or her own in the process. You may use only your spoon. When your taco shell is knocked off, you are out. Last one with the taco in place wins! And don't forget the piñata!

Spa Day: It's all about polishing, pampering, and primping at a spa party. Facials, manicures, and pedicures will keep the girls busy. Find a favorite recipe online for a homemade sugar scrub or face mask. Decorate a pair of flip-flops to wear after a pedicure. Also have a makeup station ready so they can have fun with making themselves beautiful. Maybe they could even style each other's hair. Serve triangle sandwiches and petite cakes on serving trays with smoothies or strawberry lemonade to drink!

Army Boot Camp: Get down and dirty with an action packed army training party. Decorate with American flags and anything camo. Make sure to have brown, green, and black face paint ready. Create an obstacle course for your training recruits with a balance beam, saw horse leap, and an army crawl under hung netting. Also have a tire course to run through and a tube to crawl through, with jumping jacks or pushups at the end. Fill green "grenade" water balloons for a water balloon battle! Create a target practice station using Nerf™ guns. Have MREs (ready to eat) sacks filled with army rations like popcorn, green M&M's™, beef jerky, grapes as bullets, and gumball cannon balls. For dessert, serve camo cupcakes!

RECIPES FOR FAVORITE BIRTHDAY CAKES

RED VELVET CAKE

- ½ cup shortening
- 1½ cups sugar
- 2 eggs
- 2 tsp cocoa
- 2 oz red food coloring
- 1 tsp salt
- 2¼ cups cake flour
- 1 cup buttermilk
- 1 tsp baking soda
- 1 Tbsp vinegar

Frosting:

- 1 cup milk
- 3 Tbsp flour
- 1 cup sugar
- ½ cup margarine
- ½ cup shortening
- 1 tsp vanilla

Directions:

For cake, cream ½ cup shortening and 1½ cups sugar; add eggs and salt. Mix well. Make a paste of cocoa and coloring; add to creamed mixture. Add cake flour and buttermilk alternately to the creamed mixture. Mix baking soda and vinegar together and fold slowly into batter. Bake at 350°F for 30 minutes in two 9" round pans, greased and floured.

For frosting, heat 1 cup milk and 3 tablespoons flour until thickened. Cool. Cream 1 cup sugar, margarine, and shortening together. Add vanilla. Stir in cooled flour and milk mixture and beat until smooth. Frost cake.

BUTTERFINGER™ CANDY CAKE

- One German chocolate cake mixture
- 1⅓ cup milk
- 1 box vanilla instant pudding
- 8 oz cream cheese
- 1 large carton whipped topping
- 3 Butterfinger candy bars, crushed

Directions:

Bake cake according to package directions in two 8-inch round pans. Cool. Cream the cream cheese and then add milk and pudding mix and blend together. Place one cake on dish and spread with ½ the creamed mixture. Place second cake on top and spread with remaining creamed mixture. Frost with whipped topping and cover with crushed candy bars.

If making a flat 9x13 sheetcake, spread all the creamed mixture on top of cake. Add whipped topping and cover with crushed candy bars.

CHOCOLATE BUNDT CAKE

- 1 devil's food cake mix
- 1 (3.4 oz) package instant chocolate fudge pudding and pie filling
- 1 cup sour cream (fat-free or light)
- 4 egg whites
- ½ cup warm water
- ½ cup light margarine
- 1 tsp vanilla
- 1 cup semi-sweet chocolate chips

Directions:

Preheat oven to 350°F. Stir dry ingredients together in a large mixing bowl. Add sour cream, egg whites, water, margarine, and vanilla. Beat with mixer. Stir in chocolate chips. Pour into bundt cake pan that has been sprayed with cooking spray. Bake for 40-45 minutes. Cool. Invert cooled cake on serving plate and drizzle with Powdered Sugar Glaze.

Powdered Sugar Glaze:

- 1½ cups powdered sugar
- 2 Tbsp cold milk

Directions:

Stir together in small bowl. Add more milk if needed for right consistency.

ACT IT OUT

Theme: Divide into two groups and have fun doing charades or acting out different Bible stories or characters. Have someone from the group draw out of a hat or bowl a strip of paper listing a Bible story or character. Next the group leader needs to read the account from the Bible verses listed with the names or story. Make a plan together of who will do the acting and how they should present it. Be creative and have fun! Later, reflect together on how God used these people in His plan. God sees the big picture, and He knows and allows things work together to bring glory to His name.

Verses to share and meditate on:

Psalm 40:5, *Many, Lord my God, are the wonders you have done, the things you planned for us. None can compare with you; were I to speak and tell of your deeds, they would be too many to declare.*

Psalm 103:7

Psalm 145:4–6

Jeremiah 29:11

Romans 8:28

Ephesians 3:11

Choose from these Bible stories and characters or look up your own.

Adam Names the Animals—Genesis 2:19–20

Daniel and the Lions—Daniel 16:4–23

The Wise Men Come to See Jesus—Matthew 2:1–12

Feeding the 5000—Matthew 14:14–22

Noah and the Ark—Genesis 6:14, 7:1–4

Baby Moses—Genesis 22:1–18

Ruth and Naomi—Ruth 1:6–18

David and Goliath—1 Samuel 17:23–52

Joseph and His Brothers—Genesis 37:3–5

Queen Esther before the King—Esther 5:1–2, 18–24

Moses and the Burning Bush—Exodus 3:1–6

Abraham and Isaac—Genesis 22:1–18

Lazarus Raised from the Dead—John 11:32–44

Empty Tomb in the Garden—John 20:1–18

Peter Walks on Water—Matthew 14:25–34

Jonah and the Big Fish—Jonah 1:12–2:10

Zacchaeus Climbs a Tree—Luke 19:1–10

The Shepherds See the Star—Luke 2:8–20

The Good Samaritan—Luke 10:25–37

Jesus Heals a Blind Man—Luke 18:35–43

Baby Moses in a Basket—Exodus 2:1–10

Jacob's Dream—Genesis 28:10–22

Little King Joash—2 Chronicles 24:1–11

Parable of the Lost Sheep—Luke 15:3–7

Saul Sees the Light—Acts 9:1–9

Paul and Silas Sing in Jail—Acts 16:25–32

David the Shepherd Boy—1 Samuel 16:17–19 and 17:34–37

Rebekah at the Well—Genesis 24:14–22

RECIPES:

FAVORITE KID FOODS

GRANDPA BOB'S SPAGHETTI SAUCE

- 3 (12 oz each) cans tomato paste
- 1 quart tomatoes or tomato juice
- 4 (15 oz each) cans tomato sauce
- 2 packages spaghetti sauce mix
- 1 tsp garlic powder
- ⅛ cup soy sauce
- 1 tsp Italian seasoning
- ¼ cup sugar
- ½ tsp oregano
- 2 lbs ground beef
- Optional: onions, mushrooms

Directions:

Cook ground beef; drain. Combine all ingredients and cook slowly for several hours.

CHILI

- 2 lbs ground beef
- Salt and pepper to taste
- 1 (46 oz) can tomato juice
- 1 pkg chili seasoning
- 1 cup salsa
- ½ cup brown sugar
- Optional: sour cream, grated cheddar cheese

Directions:

Brown ground beef. Season with salt and pepper. Add tomato juice, seasoning, salsa, and brown sugar. Simmer on the stove for 1 hour or longer (or use a slow cooker). Top with sour cream and grated cheddar cheese if you like.

MIDWEST CORN CHOWDER

- 1 stick margarine
- ⅓ cup flour
- 3 cups milk
- 1½ - 2 cups Velveeta™ cheese
- 2 cups cooked sliced carrots
- 3 cups cooked diced potatoes (can use bag of frozen)
- 4 cups chicken broth
- 2 cups chopped ham
- 2 cups corn

Directions:

In saucepan, melt margarine. Whisk in flour and add milk. Stir constantly and cook until thickens. Add cheese and stir until melted. Stir in the rest of the ingredients. Serve.

MACARONI AND CHEESE

- 2 cups uncooked elbow macaroni
- 2 Tbsp butter
- 2 Tbsp flour
- 1 tsp dry mustard
- 1 tsp salt
- 2 ½ cups milk
- 2 cups sharp cheddar cheese, shredded
- 1 cup Velveeta™ cheese

Directions:

Preheat oven to 375°F. Cook macaroni in 5 quarts boiling water for 8 minutes. Drain macaroni.

In medium saucepan, melt butter. Stir in flour, mustard, and salt. Gradually stir in milk. Cook and stir until mixture thickens slightly. Remove from heat. Add 1½ cups shredded cheese and Velveeta to milk mixture and stir until melted. Stir in macaroni. Turn into greased 2 quart baking dish. Top with remaining cheese. Bake 20-25 minutes or until bubbly.

BAKED CHICKEN STRIPS

- 2 boneless, skinless chicken breast halves
- 1 large egg or 2 smaller ones
- 3 cups cornflakes
- ½ tsp salt
- 1 Tbsp olive oil
- 4 Tbsp flour
- Freshly ground black pepper

Directions:

Preheat oven to 400°F and line a baking sheet with parchment paper. Rinse chicken under cold water and pat dry. Cut the chicken in long strips about ½ inch thick. Season with salt and pepper.

Beat the eggs with oil and set aside. Place the flour on a plate and set aside.

Place the cornflakes into a zip-lock bag, seal it and using a rolling pin or simply your hands, crush the cornflakes into small pieces. Put the crushed cornflakes into a flat bowl and stir in salt, pepper.

Taking one piece at a time, coat chicken strips in flour, then dip in egg mixture, and finally coat with seasoned cornflakes, pressing flakes with a fork to help them stick better. Transfer each piece onto the prepared baking sheet. Discard remaining flour, egg, and cornflakes.

Bake for about 30 minutes until golden brown and crisp, flipping them on the other side after the first 15 minutes. Serve with your favorite dipping.

BEEF STEW

- 3 lbs stew beef, cut into pieces
- Small bag of carrots, chopped
- 2 cups sweet corn
- 2 Tbsp sugar
- 1 (46 oz) can tomato juice
- Salt and pepper to taste

Directions:

Combine all ingredients in slow cooker and cook for a few hours on low.

Celebrating Life with Your Church Family

AS MEMBERS OF A CHURCH, we have a common bond together in the Lord Jesus Christ. What a privilege it is to serve each other and to work together in fulfilling the message of God's love and seeing Him honored and glorified.

WINTER RETREAT

Theme: The winter months are a good time to retreat from our busy schedules and slow down a bit. Retreat from life to meditate and reflect spiritually.

Verses to share or meditate on:

Psalm 19: 7–11, *The law of the Lord is perfect, refreshing the soul. The statutes of the Lord are trustworthy, making wise the simple. The precepts of the Lord are right, giving joy to the heart. The commands of the Lord are radiant, giving light to the eyes. The fear of the Lord is pure, enduring forever. The decrees of the Lord are firm, and all of them are righteous. They are more precious than gold, than much pure gold; they are sweeter than honey, than honey from the honeycomb. By them your servant is warned; in keeping them there is great reward.*

Psalm 18:30

Psalm 119:105

Hebrews 4:12

2 Timothy 3:15–16

Plan a fun retreat for the families in your church or group. Make sure to publicize your event. You may want to plan a theme like "Let It Snow" or "Winter Is Snow Fun." It is a great time to get away with good friends and also a time to really get to know your church family better.

Contact a church camp to see if they offer winter retreats for church or groups. The winter months are usually their time off, and they may have certain buildings you can rent for a weekend. You will probably be responsible for your own food, although some places may furnish meals for an additional price.

If you want a retreat with snow, check to see what the different areas offer at their campsites. Northern states that have snow may offer sledding, tubing, sleigh rides, cross-country skiing, or even snowmobile rentals. Kids will just enjoy playing in the snow and building snowmen and making snow angels. Try playing snow football. You will already have lots of extra padding with your snowsuit, but the snow should be soft to fall in when you are tackled! Others may enjoy playing board games together or visiting round a warm fireplace with a steamy cup of hot chocolate.

Evenings can be filled with fun games and snacks. Have a good old-fashioned sing-along and devotions from God's Word. Then retreat to your cabin and spend some quiet time alone with God. Thank Him. Praise Him. Meditate on what His Word is saying to you. Grow closer to your church family and friends and grow closer to God.

Another idea for a winter retreat is to plan a getaway just for couples. You could plan it in February around Valentine's Day and focus on marriage and family. It would be a time away without the kids—time to focus on being a couple.

Meeting sessions could be with a speaker who is asked to come and speak on marriage. There are videos that can be rented or purchased and shown during each session. For a couples retreat, you might want to look into getting rooms in a motel with a conference room and charging a fee to cover expenses. Meals would probably be on your own unless you wish to include the cost of a catered meal. It is good to spend some time together, just the two of you! Time alone will refresh your love for each other and draw you both closer to each other and to God.

RECIPES:
FOOD FOR YOUR RETREAT

CARAMEL POPCORN

- 2 bags microwave popcorn
- ½ cup margarine
- ½ cup brown sugar
- ¼ cup white corn syrup
- 1 tsp baking soda

Directions:

Pop 2 bags of microwave popcorn and put it in a big microwave safe bowl. In saucepan bring to boil the margarine, brown sugar, and white corn syrup. Boil 2 minutes. Take off heat and add 1 tsp baking soda. Stir and pour over popcorn. Microwave for three minutes, stopping and stirring at 1 minute intervals. Pour onto waxed paper.

PARTY CHEESE BALL

- 2 (8 oz) packages cream cheese, softened
- 1 (8 oz) package shredded sharp cheddar cheese
- 1 Tbsp finely chopped onion
- 1 Tbsp chopped red bell pepper
- 2 tsp Worcestershire sauce

- 1 tsp lemon juice
- Dash of red cayenne pepper
- Dash salt
- 1 cup chopped pecans

Directions:

Beat cream cheese and cheddar cheese until blended. Mix the rest of ingredients except for pecans. Shape mixture into ball and roll in pecans.

DILL PICKLE WRAPS

- Dill pickles
- Cream cheese
- Ham slices

Directions:

Spread cream cheese on slice of ham. Wrap pickle in ham. Roll up and chill. Slice in pieces ½ inch thick.

CORN DIP

- 2 cans Mexican corn
- 1 can Rotel™ tomatoes
- 1 cup mayonnaise
- 1 cup sour cream
- 5 green onions, chopped
- 12 oz shredded Mexican cheese
- 1 can green chilies, drained
- Dash of salt

Directions:

In serving bowl, mix all together.

BACON WRAPPED LITTLE SMOKIES

- Little Smokies™ cocktail sausages
- 1 package bacon
- 1 package brown sugar

Directions:

Spray a 9x13 pan with cooking spray. Wrap smokies with a 2 or 3 inch strip of bacon and secure with a toothpick. Place smokies in the pan and cover with the brown sugar. Bake at 400°F for 1 hour.

NUTCRACKER SWEETS

- 1 lb white almond bark
- 2 cups crisp rice square cereal
- 2 cups crisp corn square cereal
- 2 cups toasted oat cereal
- 1 cup pretzels
- 1 cup mixed nuts
- 1 lb M&M's™

Directions:

Combine cereals, pretzels, nuts, and M&M's in a large bowl. Melt white chocolate in microwave and pour over all to coat evenly.

HAYSTACKS

- 12 oz chocolate bark
- 1½ cups cashew nuts
- 5 oz can chow mein noodles

Directions:

Melt chocolate bark in a medium glass bowl. In separate container, combine nuts and noodles. Microwave on full power for 15 seconds. Add warmed nuts and noodles to coat. Stir until well coated. Drop by spoonfuls onto waxed paper.

TORTILLA WRAPS

- 1 package tortilla wraps
- 16 oz sour cream
- 8 oz cream cheese
- Green onion
- Black olives
- Pimentos
- Shredded cheese
- Garlic powder
- Dill weed

Directions:

Lay tortillas out flat. Mix sour cream and cream cheese with mixer. Spread on tortillas. Add remaining ingredients as desired. Roll up and slice. Refrigerate.

SPINACH DIP WITH HAWAIIAN BREAD

- 1 (10 oz) package frozen chopped spinach, cooked and drained
- 1 (8 oz) container sour cream
- ½ cup mayonnaise
- 1 small can water chestnuts, diced
- 1 package Knorr vegetable soup mix
- 3 green onions, chopped
- 1 loaf round Hawaiian bread

Directions:

Combine cooked and drained spinach, vegetable soup mix, sour cream, mayonnaise, chopped green onions, and diced water chestnuts. Mix well.

Place in airtight container and chill in refrigerator overnight to allow flavors to blend.

When ready to serve, hollow out loaf of Hawaiian bread, making a hole large enough to hold the dip. Spoon spinach dip into bread bowl and serve with remaining bread, cut into cubes.

EASY SHRIMP DIP WITH CRACKERS

- 1 (8 oz) package cream cheese, softened
- 1 (4.5 oz) can small shrimp, drained
- 1 (8 oz) jar cocktail sauce

Directions:

Spread the cream cheese on a serving platter. Then spread cocktail sauce over the cream cheese. Sprinkle with the shrimp. Refrigerate until serving. Serve with Ritz™ crackers.

A GRANDMA MINISTRY

Theme: Showing God's love by meeting the needs of widows and older ladies who are alone.

Verses to share or meditate on:

James 1:27, *Religion that God our Father accepts as pure and faultless is this: to look after orphans and widows in their distress and to keep oneself from being polluted by the world.*

1 Timothy 6:18

1 John 4:11

1 John 3:18

Colossians 3:12

1 Thessalonians 4:19

James 2:18

Matthew 5:16

One of the greatest ministries your church can have is caring for the widows or older single ladies in your church. We call it a "grandma" ministry.

Plan a party for the ladies with a theme that relates to a certain time of the year that might be extra lonely for them without a mate. One example would be Valentine's Day. Or you might plan something seasonal for spring, summer, fall, and winter.

Make each party something they look forward to by having posters made to remind them a fun event is coming soon! Make each party special by decorating and planning good food for the ladies to enjoy that relates to your theme. Also sing songs and play games with fun prizes. Have a short devotional from God's Word to complete your time together. Encourage the women to invite someone else they might know who is widowed or alone. God's Word and other Christians might be a great comfort to them.

Having a ministry like this helps make it easier for the young ladies in the church to get to know the older ladies. They will both receive a blessing and be an encouragement to one another!

There will be hugs and smiles, caring and sharing, and lots of love and laughter! What a good time to spend together in God's Word and pray for each other!

A good resource for this type of grandma ministry is "Leave the Details to Us." It has detailed parties already planned for you that include theme, decorations, recipes for food, songs, games, prizes, and a devotional relating to the theme. There are 40 fellowships divided seasonally. It can be purchased by contacting Dee Travis at dtravis56@wildblue.net.

We can bring glory to God by giving our time and talents to care for these dear ladies. What a privilege to fulfill the command of Christ found in James 1:17:

Pure and undefiled religion in the sight of our God and Father is
this: to visit orphans and widows in their distress, and to keep oneself
unstained by the world.

RECIPES:

GRASSHOPPER PIE

- 20-24 Oreo™ cookies, crushed
- 1 stick melted margarine
- Peppermint or green mint ice cream
- 8 oz jar of hot fudge sauce
- 8 oz Cool Whip™
- Andes™ mints

Directions:

Crush Oreos and put into 9x13 pan. Pour melted butter over top. Freeze for one hour. Top crumbs with ice cream. Warm hot fudge sauce for about 30 seconds and drizzle over ice cream. Freeze! Spread Cool Whip on top like frosting. Sprinkle with shaved Andes mints.

BERRIED DELIGHT

- 1½ cups graham cracker crumbs
- ¼ cup sugar
- ⅓ cup melted margarine
- 8 oz cream cheese, softened
- ¼ cup sugar
- 2 Tbsp milk
- 2 cups Cool Whip™
- 2 pints fresh strawberries
- 2 small packages instant vanilla pudding
- 3½ cups milk
- 8 oz Cool Whip (for topping)

Directions:

Combine crumbs, sugar and margarine. Press into a 9x13 pan. Chill 15 minutes. Beat cream cheese, sugar, and milk until smooth. Fold in Cool Whip. Spread over crust. Top with strawberries, hulled and halved. Prepare pudding with the 3½ cups milk. Pour over berries. Chill several hours or overnight. Before serving, add more Cool Whip on top of pudding. Garnish with strawberries, if desired. *Serves 15.*

PEANUT BUTTER CREAM CHEESE DELIGHT

- 1½ cups vanilla wafers, crushed
- ½ cup peanuts, chopped
- ¼ cup butter or margarine, melted
- 2 Tbsp chunky peanut butter
- 2 (8 oz) packages cream cheese, softened
- ¼ cup sugar
- ½ cup chunky peanut butter
- 2 tsp vanilla
- 4 eggs
- 2 cups whipping cream or 4 cups Cool Whip™
- ¾ cup thick chocolate fudge ice cream topping

Directions:

Combine cookies, peanuts, butter, and peanut butter. Blend until crumbly. Press 1 cup crumb mixture into bottom of a 12-cup fluted tube pan. Combine cream cheese, sugar, 2 cups peanut butter, and vanilla. Beat 3 minutes at high speed. Beat in eggs, one at a time. Fold in whipped cream. Spoon half of cheese mixture over crumbs in pan. Drop fudge topping by 8 spoonfuls over cheese mixture, then add remaining cheese mixture. Marble by cutting through with table knife in an over-and-under fashion, almost through to the bottom. Smooth top. Sprinkle with remaining crumbs; press lightly. Freeze. *Makes 12-14 servings.*

TRIPLE BERRY DESSERT

- 2 cans cherry pie filling
- 2 cups blueberries
- 2 cups red raspberries
- 1½ cups sugar
- 3 Tbsp flour

Directions:
Mix together and pour in a greased 9x13 pan.

Topping:

- 2 cups flour
- 2 cups brown sugar
- 1 cup margarine

Directions:
Cut together flour, brown sugar, and margarine. Crumble on top of fruit batter. Bake at 375°F for 35-45 minutes or until bubbling around the edges.

VALENTINE OUTREACH

Theme: To let others know how much God loves them and what He has done for them through His Son.

Verses to share and meditate on:

John 15:12–13, *My command is this: Love each other as I have loved you. Greater love has no one than this: to lay down one's life for one's friends.*

John 13:34

Genesis 2:24

1 Corinthians 13:13

1 John 4:10, 12

1 John 4:1–8

John 3:16

Celebrate Valentine's Day with a couple's banquet or dinner out in a restaurant. The goal is to invite friends who need to hear the message of God's great love. Often you can rent a conference or banquet room in a motel or restaurant. Sometimes people will say yes to an invitation when the event isn't in a church. When you invite them, tell them that their meal is on you, if that is feasible for you.

Another option would be to have your dinner at church in your fellowship area and have the meal catered. You can decorate in valentine colors, have candlelight, and play soft music to make it special.

Begin by planning a date close to Valentine's Day but not the weekend you think most people will be celebrating, or you will lose couples and available restaurants. The weekend ahead might work well.

Look for a restaurant with a meeting or conference room. Check out the food menu and prices. Sometimes you can get a better price by promising a certain amount of people or if you select only two or three main courses on the menu. Also ask if you can bring chocolate candies or red confetti hearts to add to the center of each table as decorations.

If finances allow, make sure to have some door prizes or a little something for each couple to take home. Some ideas for door prizes would be:

> A heart-shaped box of chocolates
> A red valentine candle
> Christian CD with love songs
> Gift certificate for a hot fudge sundae for two

Add a romantic and fun atmosphere by utilizing talent from your church to play soft music on a keyboard or find violin players to serenade the tables. You can always play a nice romantic CD as background music.

Put together a men's quartet from your church and ask them to sing some old love songs as a special. Another idea would be to play

"Name that Tune" with old love songs and see which couple get the most right.

Examples:

1. *What the World Needs Now Is Love Sweet Love*
2. *When Love Shines In*
3. *Love Me Tender*
4. *Roses Are Red, My Love*
5. *If Ever I Would Leave You*
6. *Love Is a Many Splendored Thing*
7. *L-O-V-E*
8. *Love and Marriage*
9. Theme from *Love Story*

Skits are another fun activity if you have willing people!

You will also want to secure a speaker well in advance of the date, perhaps someone from within your church family. Make sure they know it is an outreach to unsaved friends.

Most of all, as a church body be praying for people to have open hearts to the gospel. What a good time of year to let others know how much God loves and cares for them.

RECIPES:

CHERRY CHEESECAKE

- 12 graham crackers
- ¼ cup sugar
- 6 Tbsp margarine
- 1 (8 oz) package cream cheese

- 1 Tbsp milk
- 1 tsp vanilla
- 1 cup sifted powdered sugar
- 8 oz Cool Whip™
- 1 can cherry pie filling

Directions:

Mix crackers, sugar, and margarine. Put in pie pan. Bake at 300°F for 5-7 minutes. Soften cheese, and add milk, vanilla, and powdered sugar. Blend well. Add Cool Whip, and then spread on crust and chill. When firm, spoon on can of cherry pie filling. *Serves 12.*

ICE CREAM BROWNIE SUNDAE DESSERT

- 1 large box brownie mix
- ½ gallon vanilla ice cream
- 1-2 cups salted peanuts

Directions:

Bake brownie mix according to directions. Cool. Spread vanilla ice cream over brownies. Cover with salted peanuts. Freeze.

Topping:

- 2 cups chocolate chips
- 2 cups powdered sugar
- 1 cup evaporated milk
- ½ cup margarine

Directions:

Mix ingredients in a medium-sized saucepan. Bring to a boil and boil 8 minutes. Add 1 tsp vanilla. Cool ½ hour. Pour over frozen dessert. Return to freezer.

SUGAR COOKIES

- 1 cup margarine
- 1 cup sugar
- 3 eggs
- 3¾ cups flour
- ½ tsp salt
- ½ tsp baking soda
- 2 tsp cream of tartar
- 1½ tsp vanilla

Directions:

Cream together margarine and sugar. Add eggs and blend well. In a separate bowl, sift together flour, salt, soda, and cream of tartar. Gradually add flour mixture to creamed mixture. Mix in vanilla; chill dough thoroughly (at least 1 hour).

Roll chilled dough on floured surface and cut into heart-shaped cookies. Bake at 375°F for 8 minutes. Frost with red, pink, and white frosting and decorate with holiday sprinkles.

STRAWBERRY JUNKET DESSERT

First Layer:

- 1 cup powdered sugar
- 8 oz cream cheese, softened
- 1 small tub Cool Whip™, thawed
- 1 angel food cake, cubed

Topping:

- 1 box Junket Danish Dessert™, Strawberry Flavor (a strawberry pie filling glaze)
- 2 cups water

- 2 cups frozen, sweetened strawberries (thawed) or 4 cups fresh strawberries

Directions:

Cream together powdered sugar and cream cheese. Fold in Cool Whip and add angel food cake. Mix well. Pour into a rectangular cake pan, and spread evenly.

In a saucepan, stir 2 cups cold water into the junket mix. Bring to a boil, stirring constantly. Boil for 1 minute. Stir in strawberries. Pour filling over bottom layer. Chill for 3 hours before serving.

SPRING PICK-ME-UP

Theme: Being willing to help and encourage others with our time and a little physical labor.

Verses to share and meditate on:

Hebrews 4:16, *Let us then approach God's throne of grace with confidence, so that we may receive mercy and find grace to help us in our time of need.*

Psalm 33:20

Psalm 46:1

Psalm 121:1

Hebrews 3:13

1 Thessalonians 5:11

This is a great ministry as a church to be able to help others with their spring yard work. It will also be a time together to fellowship and have some fun.

To start, get a list of names from your church family or neighborhood of people who might be in need of some help. It might be an elderly couple, single lady, or single young mother, or it could be someone who has been sick or injured and is unable to do this type of physical work. Maybe someone has an unsaved friend or neighbor who could use a helping hand. This would open up a chance to talk to them about the Lord.

Make sure to contact the people you have chosen to help ahead of time, and be sure they would welcome the help and ask what they would like your workers to do. It might be raking the yard or washing windows or painting a fence! Then set a time for a group of workers to be there.

The day of your "spring pick-me-up," have everyone meet at the church and divide into groups. Then, hand out assignments of what needs done at each home. Ask people to bring tools they might need for outside work, such as rakes, trash bags, and paint brushes. Be sure to include the whole family where possible. There may be kids who are big enough to help with jobs such as picking up sticks. Have a good time with each other and be considerate as you work so your good works bring glory to God!

If it is possible, spend a little time with the people you are helping. Perhaps someone could bake them some homemade cookies or bars and take them a plate. Let them know you care about them and are happy to help out. It might even turn into an opportunity to share your faith with them.

There may be some church folks who want to help but are not physically able. Offer them the opportunity of preparing lunch or snacks to take along or have a meal ready back at the church later in the day.

It might be fun to use the sticks and leaves you have all picked up for a hot dog roast—if you had the right time and place!

Planning ahead and acquiring lots of help is the key. You might want to have sign-up sheets a week or two ahead so you will know how many volunteers you have and what each can do to serve. Some might even sign up to pray for the activities of the day, and that it would be a good day of ministry and encouragement the lives of other people.

RECIPES FOR BARS:

DREAM BARS

- ¾ cup brown sugar
- ¾ cup butter
- 1½ cups flour
- 1½ cups brown sugar
- ¾ tsp baking powder
- 3 eggs, beaten
- ½ tsp salt
- 1½ tsp vanilla
- 3 Tbsp flour
- 2 cups coconut

Directions:

Mix first three ingredients until crumbly. Pat into 8x10 pan and bake at 350°F for 10 minutes. Combine the remaining ingredients. Spread on top of baked crust. Bake 20-25 minutes at 350°F.

CHOCOLATE REVEL BARS

- 1 cup shortening
- 2 cups brown sugar
- 2 eggs
- 2½ cups flour
- 1 tsp baking soda
- 1 tsp salt

- 2 tsp vanilla
- 3 cups quick oatmeal
- 1 (12 oz) package chocolate chips
- 1 can Eagle Brand™ condensed milk
- 2 tsp vanilla
- 2 Tbsp butter
- ½ tsp salt

Directions:

Cream shortening and sugar, add eggs, and mix. Add flour, baking soda, salt, vanilla, and oatmeal. Spread ⅔ cup of oatmeal mixture in jelly roll pan. Melt chips, milk, vanilla, butter and salt over low heat. Spread over oatmeal mixture. Spread or dot with remaining oatmeal mixture. Bake 25-30 minutes at 350°F. Let cool and cut into bars.

PEANUT BUTTER FINGERS

- ½ cup butter
- ½ cup sugar
- ½ cup brown sugar
- 1 egg
- ⅓ cup peanut butter
- ½ tsp baking soda
- ¼ tsp salt
- 1 cup flour
- ½ tsp vanilla
- 1 cup oatmeal
- ½ cup powdered sugar
- ¼ cup peanut butter
- 2-4 Tbsp milk

Directions:

Cream butter and sugars. Add egg and peanut butter. Mix together soda, salt, and flour and add to creamed mixture. Add vanilla and stir in oatmeal. Bake in 9x13 pan at 350°F for 20-25 minutes. Sprinkle with 1 cup chocolate chips as soon as it is out of oven. Let stand 5 minutes and spread. Combine powdered sugar, peanut butter, and milk and drizzle over the top. Cut into bars.

CHERRY BARS

- 1 cup butter
- 1¾ cups sugar
- 4 eggs
- 1 tsp vanilla
- 3 cups flour
- ½ tsp baking powder
- ½ tsp salt
- 1 or 2 cans cherry pie filling

Directions:

Cream butter and sugar. Add eggs, then vanilla. Add flour, baking powder, and salt. Pat ⅔ of mixture in greased cookie sheet. Spread filling over. Spread remaining batter on top. Bake 350°F 45 minutes. Let cool 10 minutes. Frost with powdered sugar frosting.

SPRING PING

Theme: Spring is the time when new life begins. There is new green grass, new flowers, and in the spring new baby animals are born. They can remind us of our new life in Christ.

Verses to share and meditate on:

2 Corinthians 5:17, *Therefore, if anyone is in Christ, the new creation has come: The old has gone, the new is here!*

1 John 2:25

1 John 5:13

John 3:16

Romans 6:4

This is a fun church activity for your whole church family. People at any age love to play ping-pong. Check with your local school or YMCA to see if you can rent their gym and ping-pong tables. Some churches may have a big enough fellowship hall to set up a few tables in their own church.

You will need to post a sign-up sheet to find out who is interested in playing. Divide your sign-up sheet into different ages. Then you will need to organize and place brackets for your tournament. Make it a single or a double elimination tournament. You could have some fun with this and seed the entries, also giving them funny nicknames like the Dave "The Dominator" or "Fast and Furious" Fred. This will be fun, especially if you announce the nicknames before they play their games.

Have fun prizes for the winners. You could have the over all winner, the loudest player, the best server, etc.

After or during the tourney, have food such as grilled hotdogs, chips, and bars or cookies. You could also order pizzas and take up a free will offering. A devotional could be shared about springing/pinging into the spring season and being ready and on our feet for each opportunity God brings us!

RECIPES:

CHEWY BROWNIE BARS

- 2 cups sugar
- 4 eggs
- 1 cup oil
- 2 Tbsp light corn syrup
- 1½ cups flour
- ⅓ cup cocoa
- ½ tsp salt
- 1 tsp baking powder
- 1 tsp vanilla

Directions:

Preheat oven to 350°F. Combine sugar, flour, cocoa, salt, baking powder. Combine oil, eggs, corn syrup, and vanilla. Add to dry ingredients. Spread in 9x13 pan. Bake for 25 minutes or until toothpick inserted in center comes out clean. Dust with powdered sugar while warm.

PECAN PIE BARS

- 2⅔ cups flour
- 2½ sticks margarine, softened
- 1¼ cups brown sugar
- 2 cups pecans, chopped
- 1 cup white corn syrup
- 1 cup sugar
- 1½ tsp vanilla
- ¼ tsp salt
- 6 eggs

Directions:
Preheat oven to 350°F. Make crust by mixing flour, brown sugar, and margarine. Press into a 11x16 jelly roll pan. Bake 10 minutes. Mix eggs, sugar, syrup, vanilla, and pecans together. Pour over partially baked crust. Bake 40 minutes at 325°F or until consistency of pecan pie.

HEATH™ BRICKLE BLONDE BROWNIES

- 1½ cups flour
- 2 tsp baking powder
- ½ tsp salt
- ½ cup margarine
- 1 cup sugar
- ½ cup brown sugar
- 2 eggs
- 1 tsp vanilla
- 1 package Heath Bits o' Brickle™ chips

Directions:

Stir flour, baking powder, and salt together. Cream margarine. Add both sugars and cream well. Add the eggs and vanilla; beat until fluffy. Blend in dry ingredients. Stir in Heath Bits o' Brickle chips. Spread over bottom of well-greased 9x13 pan. Bake at 350°F about 30 minutes or until done. Cool and cut into bars 1x3. *Makes 15 bars.*

FROSTED BANANA BARS

- ½ cup butter or margarine, softened
- 1½ cups sugar
- 2 eggs
- 1 cup sour cream
- 1 tsp vanilla
- 2 cups flour
- 1 tsp baking soda
- ¼ tsp salt
- 2 medium ripe bananas, mashed

Directions:

Preheat oven to 350°F. Cream butter and sugar. Add eggs, sour cream and vanilla. Combine flour, baking soda, and salt, gradually adding to the creamed mixture. Stir in bananas. Spread on a greased jelly roll pan. Bake for 20-25 minutes or until a tooth pick inserted near the center comes out clean. Cool.

Frosting:

- 8 oz cream cheese, softened
- ½ cup butter or margarine, softened
- 2 tsp vanilla extract
- 3¾-4 cups powdered sugar

Directions:

Beat cream cheese, butter, and vanilla. Gradually beat in enough powdered sugar to achieve desired consistency. Frost bars. Store in the refrigerator. *Makes 48 bars.*

SUMMER STRAWBERRY EXTRAVAGANZA

Theme: Praising God with harmonious singing and celebrating life with song, strawberries, and shortcake. Live in harmony with one another.

Verses to share and meditate on:

Psalm 33:1-3, *Sing joyfully to the Lord, you righteous; it is fitting for the upright to praise him. Praise the Lord with the harp; make music to him on the ten-stringed lyre. Sing to him a new song; play skillfully, and shout for joy.*

Psalm 100:2

Psalm 96:1

Psalm 40:3

James 5:13

Colossians 3:16

Hebrews 13:15

Ephesians 5:19

Who can resist fresh red strawberries spooned over shortcake and topped with ice cream? The best time of year for this event would be during fresh strawberry season, but frozen strawberries will work great too. Large groups might want to check into large three-five gallon pails of frozen berries.

You will also need to purchase gallons of ice cream, bowls, napkin, and spoons. Ask ladies of the church to provide short cakes, yellow cakes, or angel food cakes. Red and white table cloths will add fun and color to your room. Use red and white stripes if possible to go with the barber shop theme. If you want to get creative and make barber shop poles, you could paint PVC pipe with red stripes or wrap them with red crepe paper.

Top off the evening with a good old-fashioned men's barber shop quartet. Some of the hymns they could sing a cappella and harmonize with might include:

1. *Nothing but the Blood*
2. *Victory in Jesus*
3. *God Is so Good*
4. *Amazing Grace*
5. *When We All Get to Heaven*
6. *Leaning on the Everlasting Arms*
7. *Standing on the Promises*
8. *Just Over in Gloryland*
9. *The Old Rugged Cross*
10. *I Will Sing the Wondrous Story*
11. *Wonderful Words of Life*

If you have your event in June/July, use a patriotic theme and have the men sing songs accordingly.

Examples:

1. *God Bless America*
2. *Stars and Stripes Forever*
3. *The Star-Spangled Banner*
4. *America the Beautiful*
5. *This Is My Country*
6. *Battle Hymn of the Republic*

This fellowship could be planned on a Sunday evening after church and could be used to swing into the summer quarter. It could also be a lead-in to Vacation Bible School week; workers could get together afterward to organize and decorate rooms for an upcoming week of Bible school. It could also be an after-church Father's Day celebration.

RECIPES:

ANGEL FOOD CAKE

- 1¼ cups cake flour, sifted
- ½ cup sugar, sifted
- 2 cups egg whites, room temperature (10-12 eggs)
- ¼ tsp salt
- 1¼ tsp cream of tartar
- 1 tsp vanilla
- ¼ tsp almond extract
- 1⅓ cups sifted sugar

Directions:

Sift flour; then measure 1¼ cups of it. Add ½ cup sifted sugar to the flour and sift together four times. Set aside. Combine egg whites, salt, cream of tartar, vanilla, and almond extract. Beat with a mixer until the whites form soft peaks. Add the rest of the sugar (1⅓ cups) in four additions, about 5 Tbsp at a time. Beat with a wire whisk, 25 strokes after each addition. Add flour in 4 parts and beat with wire whisk, 15 strokes after each addition. Pour into an ungreased angel food cake pan. Bake at 350°F for about 40 minutes. Remove cake from oven. Invert pan; cool at least 1 hour. Loosen sides with knife before removing.

HOMEMADE ICE CREAM

- 4 eggs
- 2½ cups sugar
- 1 quart half-and-half
- ½ gallon milk
- 1 Tbsp vanilla
- 1 tsp lemon extract
- 1 tsp salt
- 2 packages dry Dream Whip™

Directions:

Beat eggs until light. Gradually add sugar; blend until thick. Add half-and-half, milk, vanilla, lemon extract, salt, and Dream Whip. Mix well and freeze.

POUND CAKE

- 1 lb butter, softened
- 3 cups sugar
- 6 large eggs
- 4 cups all-purpose flour
- ¾ cup milk
- 1 tsp almond extract
- 1 tsp vanilla extract

Directions:

Preheat oven to 300°F. Beat butter at medium speed with an electric mixer until creamy. (The butter will become a lighter yellow color; this is an important step, as the job of the mixer is to incorporate air into the butter so the cake will rise. It will take 1-7 minutes, depending on the power of your mixer.) Gradually add sugar, beating at medium speed until light and fluffy. (Again, the times will vary, and butter will turn to a fluffy white.) Add eggs, 1 at a time, beating just until yellow yolk disappears.

Add flour to creamed mixture alternately with milk, beginning and ending with flour. Beat at low speed just until blended after each addition. Stir in extracts.

Pour into a greased and floured 10-inch tube pan. (Use vegetable shortening or butter to grease the pan, getting every nook and cranny covered. Sprinkle a light coating of flour over the greased surface.)

Bake for 1 hour and 40 minutes or until a long wooden pick inserted in center comes out clean. Cool in pan on a wire rack 10-15 minutes. Remove from pan, and cool completely on a wire rack.

STRAWBERRY SHORTCAKE

- 3 pints fresh strawberries
- ½ cup white sugar
- 2¼ cups all-purpose flour
- 4 tsp baking powder
- 2 Tbsp white sugar
- ¼ tsp salt
- ⅓ cup shortening
- 1 egg

- ⅔ cup milk
- 2 cups whipped heavy cream

Directions:

Slice the strawberries and toss them with ½ cup of white sugar. Set aside.

Preheat oven to 425°F. Grease and flour one 8 inch round cake pan. In a medium bowl combine the flour, baking powder, 2 Tbsp white sugar, and the salt. With a pastry blender, cut in the shortening until the mixture resembles coarse crumbs. Make a well in the center and add the beaten egg and milk. Stir until just combined. Spread the batter into the prepared pan. Bake for 15-20 minutes or until golden brown. Let cool partially in pan on wire rack.

Slice partially cooled cake in half, making two layers. Place half of the strawberries on one layer and top with the other layer. Top with remaining strawberries and cover with the whipped cream. *Makes one 8-inch round cake*

MOTHER/DAUGHTER FELLOWSHIP

Theme: A fun fellowship honoring mothers and daughters or ladies and friends of any age.

Verses to share and meditate on:

1 John 1:7, *But if we walk in the light, as he is in the light, we have fellowship with one another, and the blood of Jesus, his Son, purifies us from all sin.*

Philippians 2:1–2

Philippians 3:10

2 Corinthians 13:14

Psalm 55:14

Galatians 2:9

Mother/Daughter fellowships are great anytime but are usually held around Mother's Day. Mothers and daughters enjoy fun activities they can do together! This is also a good outreach event. If your mother or daughter is unable to come or you are single—adopt someone to come with you!

Start by organizing a committee. Select a theme, date and time, and location for your event.

Here are some examples of themes you might enjoy:

1. Come for Coffee – Let's Talk
2. Heavenly Handbags – What We Carry with Us
3. How about a Makeover? Inner Beauty
4. How Does Your Garden Grow? Growing with God
5. It Takes Two – Mom and Me
6. Let's Go Shopping – Life Has Choices
7. Old-Fashioned Baskets – Ways Women Use Them
8. Queen for a Day – We are Royalty
9. Strawberry Brunch – Bearing One Another's Burdens
10. Sugar and Spice – Our Fragrance to God

These ideas are taken from *Let's Plan a Party*[1] resource party planning book available through Regular Baptist Press bookstore. It gives you everything for planning these fellowships. It has theme and decoration ideas, food and recipes, songs, games and prizes to go with the theme, name tags, outlines, and a devotional.

RECIPES:

SNICKERDOODLE MUFFINS

- 1 cup butter
- 1 cup sugar
- 2 eggs
- 1¼ cups flour
- ¼ tsp baking powder
- ¼ tsp cream of tartar
- 1 cup sour cream
- ¼ cup buttermilk

1   Travis, Dee, and Lynne Reeves. *Let's Plan a Party: 40 Creative Ideas for Special Programs in Your Church*. Schaumburg, Ill.: Regular Baptist Press, 2004.

Topping:

- ½ cup sugar
- 2 Tbsp cinnamon

Directions:

Preheat oven to 350°F. Combine dry ingredients. Cream shortening and sugar, and add egg. Stir in dry ingredients. Beat smooth after each addition. Roll chunks of dough in topping and place in muffin tin. When muffins are in the tins, sprinkle a little more topping on each one. Bake 15 to 18 minutes.

SCONES

- 1¾ cup flour
- ¼ cup sugar
- 4 tsp baking powder
- ⅛ tsp salt
- 5 Tbsp cold butter, cut up
- ½ cup plus 1 Tbsp milk
- ¼ cup sour cream or plain yogurt
- ⅓ cup dried cranberries
- 3 Tbsp orange zest
- 1 egg slightly beaten

Directions:

Preheat oven to 400°F. Mix flour, sugar, baking powder, and salt. Cut in butter to form loose crumbs. Stir together ½ cup milk, sour cream or yogurt, zest, and cranberries. Stir into flour mixture until moistened and holding together. Transfer dough to lightly floured surface and pat into a rectangle. Knead a few times and form into a rectangle again that is ¾ inch thick. Cut into 8 triangles. Place on a parchment lined pan. Whisk eggs and 1 Tbsp milk together and brush on the top of each scone. Bake for 15 minutes or until golden brown.

APPLESAUCE OAT MUFFINS

- 1 cup rolled oats
- 1 cup applesauce
- ½ cup milk
- 1 egg
- 1 tsp vanilla
- 4 Tbsp butter or coconut oil
- ⅓ cup sugar
- ¾ cup whole-wheat flour
- 1 tsp baking powder
- ½ tsp baking soda
- 1 tsp cinnamon
- ¼ tsp salt
- ½ cup raisins or dried cranberries

Directions:

Preheat oven to 375°F. Stir together applesauce, oatmeal, milk, egg, vanilla, butter, and sugar. Set aside.

In large bowl whisk flour, baking powder, baking soda, salt, cinnamon, and raisins or cranberries. Make a well in the center and pour in the applesauce mixture. Stir until just blended. Put in muffin tins and bake for 15-20 minutes. *Makes 12 servings*.

CINNAMON CRUNCH MUFFINS

- 3 cups flour
- 1½ cups brown sugar, firmly packed
- 2 tsp cinnamon, divided

- ½ tsp salt
- 1 tsp ground ginger
- ½ cup shortening
- 1 tsp baking powder
- ½ tsp baking soda
- 2 eggs, beaten
- 1 cup buttermilk
- ½ cup chopped pecans

Directions:

In a large bowl, stir together flour, sugar, 1 tsp cinnamon, salt, and ginger. Add shortening; mix until crumbly. Put ⅔ cup of flour mixture into a small bowl. Add 1 tsp cinnamon and pecans. Set aside to use for the topping. Add baking powder and baking soda to the remaining mixture; stir well. Add eggs and buttermilk; stir just until blended. Spoon batter into buttered muffin tins, filling each cup about ⅔ full. Sprinkle muffins with the reserved topping. Bake at 350°F for 15-20 minutes.

POPPY SEED MUFFINS

- 1½ cups flour
- ½ cup wheat germ
- ⅓ cup poppy seeds
- ⅓ cup sugar
- 1 Tbsp baking powder
- ½ tsp salt
- 1 cup milk
- 1 egg
- ¼ cup unsalted butter, melted

Directions:

Preheat oven to 400°F. In a large bowl, stir together flour, wheat germ, poppy seeds, sugar, baking powder, and salt. Set aside.

In a small bowl, whisk together milk, egg, and butter until smooth. Add to dry ingredients and stir just until blended. Spoon into buttered muffin tins, filling each cup about ⅔ full. Bake for 15-18 minutes.

ZUCCHINI NUT MUFFINS

- 1 cup shredded zucchini
- 2 eggs
- 2 tsp vanilla
- 1 tsp cinnamon
- ½ cup oil
- ½ cup walnuts
- 1 cup flour
- 1 cup sugar
- ¾ tsp baking soda
- ½ tsp salt
- ⅛ tsp baking powder

Directions:

Preheat oven to 400°F. Mix zucchini, eggs, vanilla, oil, and walnuts. Sift together dry ingredients and add to mixture a little at a time. Beat until just blended. Bake for 18 minutes.

MORNING GLORY MUFFINS

- 2 cups flour
- ¾ cup sugar

- 1 tsp baking soda (dissolved in 1 Tbsp water)
- 2 tsp cinnamon
- 2 cups grated carrots
- 1 apple, chopped
- ½ cup raisins
- ½ cup pecans
- ½ cup coconut
- 3 eggs
- ½ cup margarine, melted
- 2 tsp vanilla

Directions:

In a medium bowl, mix all ingredients together. Fill muffin tin ⅔ full with batter. Bake at 325°F for 15 to 18 minutes.

FATHER/SON EVENTS

Theme: Fathers and sons and men of all ages enjoying time spent together. It is a good time to reflect on our personal relationships with one another and also our personal relationship with God as our Father.

Verses to share and meditate on:

Exodus 20:12, *Honor your father and your mother, so that you may live long in the land the Lord your God is giving you.*

Proverbs 1:8

Proverbs 10:1

John 10:30

Matthew 3:17

John 3:16

1 John 5:12

Romans 8:32

John 3:35

Father/Son events are a great time for spending time with each other, but it is also a good event to use as an outreach to your neighbors and those in your community. Plan fun and unique parties that guys will feel comfortable inviting unsaved men and their sons to attend.

Start by organizing a committee and ask them to select a theme, date and time, and location for this event. Most men enjoy outdoor activities, and as an outreach, visitors might be more agreeable about coming if this event isn't held in a church.

Here are some ideas you might like to use.

1. Back on the Farm – The Prodigal Son
2. Blazing a Trail Cowboys – Men of Faith (Hebrews)
3. Camping with Dad – Abraham and Isaac
4. Cars, Trucks, and Chariots – Trust in God
5. Goals for Life – Put on God's Equipment
6. Harvest Of Souls – Faith of a Farmer
7. Home Improvement – Tools in God's Hands
8. Hook, Line, and Sinker – Be Fishers of Men
9. Mountain Men – The Strength of Samson
10. Take Me Out to the Ballgame – Be a Winner/ Finish Strong

These ideas are taken from *Let's Plan a Party*[2] resource party planning book available through Regular Baptist Press bookstore(http://www.rbpstore.org). It gives you everything for planning these fellowships. It has theme and decoration ideas, food and recipes, songs, games and prizes to go with the theme, name tags, outlines, and a devotional.

RECIPES:

HAM BALLS
- 1 lb ground beef
- 1 lb ground pork

---

2   Ibid.

- 2 lb ground ham
- 2 cups graham cracker crumbs
- 3 eggs
- 2 cups milk
- ½ tsp pepper
- 1 tsp salt
- 1 tsp onion salt

Topping:

- 1 cup ketchup
- 2 cups brown sugar
- 2 tsps mustard
- ½ cup plus 4 Tbsp vinegar
- 1 cup water

Directions:

Mix ham ball ingredients together. Shape into medium-sized balls. In another bowl, mix topping ingredients together. Pour topping over ham balls and bake at 350°F for one hour or until done. *Makes 24 servings*.

BRISKET

- One 12-15 pound cooked brisket

Sauce:

- 1 Tbsp meat tenderizer
- 1 bottle liquid smoke
- 1 Tbsp celery salt
- 1 Tbsp paprika
- 1 Tbsp garlic powder

- 1 Tbsp onion salt
- 3 Tbsp brown sugar

Directions:

Mix sauce in a saucepan and bring to a boil until spices dissolve. Place cooked brisket in a large baking pan with 1 inch sides. Pour sauce over brisket and cover with foil. Cook in preheated 350°F oven for 1½ hours or until heated thoroughly.

FRUIT PIZZA

- 1½ cups butter or margarine
- ½ cup vegetable shortening
- 1 cup sugar
- 1 egg
- ½ tsp vanilla
- 2 cups flour
- ½ tsp cream of tartar
- ½ tsp baking soda
- ¼ tsp salt
- 2 (8 oz) packages cream cheese, softened
- 1 cup powdered sugar
- 1 cup Cool Whip™, thawed
- 1 cup pineapple juice
- 1 cup orange juice
- 2 Tbsp corn starch
- Assorted fruit

Directions:

Cream together butter, shortening, and sugar. Add egg and vanilla. Combine dry ingredients and add to creamed mixture.

Press dough into cookie sheet with sides. Bake at 350°F for 8-10 minutes until slightly brown. Cool.

Whip cream cheese until smooth. Add sugar and whipped topping. Spread over crust. In a saucepan, cook juices and cornstarch. Stir until thick. Reserve 2 cups of glaze. Spread remaining lukewarm glaze over cream cheese filling. Then add fruits: raspberries, kiwis, bananas, mandarin oranges, pineapple chunks, strawberries, grapes. Drizzle or brush on remaining glaze over fruit. Chill.

BANANA SPLIT CAKE

- 1½ cups vanilla wafers, crushed
- ½ cup margarine
- 8 oz cream cheese
- 2 Tbsp milk
- 1 cup sugar
- 1 can crushed pineapple, drained
- 2 or more bananas
- 1 large Cool Whip™

Directions:

Mix wafer crumbs and margarine. Press into 9x13 pan and bake for 5 minutes at 350°F. Cool. In mixing bowl, mix cream cheese, sugar, and milk and spread over crust. Add a layer of bananas. Add a layer of pineapple. Top with Cool Whip. *Makes 12 servings.*

BABY SHOWERS

Theme: Celebrating the new life of a new baby can remind us of new life in Christ.

Verses to share and meditate on:

Psalm 127:3, *Children are a heritage from the Lord, offspring a reward from him.*

Proverbs 22:6

Ephesians 6:46

Deuteronomy 6:7

Proverbs 20:7

Matthew 19:13–14

3 John 4

Excitement surrounds a new baby. They are sweet, soft, precious little miracles from God! Mom, dad, grandparents, and all of us want to help celebrate and thank God for the safe arrival of their bundle of joy. As a church family, we want to encourage new moms and dads by showering them with gifts for their new little one.

Take time to reflect on the fact that the most precious gift was sent from heaven by God as a baby. It was His Son, Jesus Christ. God sent Him as a gift to us to bring us the gift of eternal life!

Here are a few ideas you might like to use:

1. A Special Gift from God – God's Gift to Us

2. Baby Farm Animals – New Life in Christ

3. Jesus Loves Me – The Good Shepherd and His Little Sheep

4. I Love My Teddy Bear – Safe and Secure

5. Noah's Zoo – God's Promises

6. Baby, Beautiful Baby of Mine – Ours for a Time

7. Precious Moments and Sweet Dreams – Prayer Time

8. Rock-a-Bye Baby – Rest in the Lord

9. Tiny Hands to Hold – God's Almighty Hands

10. Toy Chest – Train Up a Child

Start with organizing a committee and choosing a chair person to be in charge. These are some of the areas you will need to include:

1. Date and Time: Check with honoree for date and time that works. Ask if they would prefer a shower before or after the baby is born.

2. Announcement and Invitations: You will need to put details of the shower in the church bulletin and ask the honoree if there is anyone outside of the church family that she might like you to send an invitation to. Have her give you a list with addresses. Make sure to do this a couple of weeks before the event.

3. Gift and Card: Have one person on the committee who will check registries and purchase the committee gift.

4. Bulletin Boards: If you have a bulletin board in the room where your shower is to be held, be sure to decorate it. You could use pictures of the new baby or pictures of the mom and dad-to-be when they were babies!

5. Decorations: Decorate with a baby theme. If you know the baby is a boy or a girl, decorate accordingly.

6. Food committee: Find out what are some of the mothers favorite foods or if there is something she can't eat.

7. Paper Items: Purchase plates, napkins, and cups to go with your baby theme.

8. Music: Choose a few songs to sing about new life or have soft lullaby music in the background as people arrive.

9. Games and Prizes: Find fun games and prizes you know the honoree will enjoy.

10. Devotional: Ask someone who knows the couple to share some encouraging thoughts on parenting from God's Word.

These ideas are taken from *Let's Plan a Party*[3] resource party planning book available through Regular Baptist Press bookstore. It gives you everything for planning these fellowships. It has theme and decoration ideas, food and recipes, songs, games and prizes to go with the theme, name tags, outlines, and a devotional. The CD included lets you copy the games, assignment sheet, week-by-week responsibilities, and much more!

RECIPES:

CHUBBY CHEEKS CHOCOLATE DESSERT

- 1 cup flour
- ½ cup margarine
- ¼ cup chopped pecans
- 1 (8 oz) package cream cheese

---

3   Ibid.

- 1 cup Cool Whip™
- 1 cup powdered sugar
- 2 packages instant chocolate pudding
- 1 tsp vanilla
- 3 cups milk

Directions:

First layer: combine flour, margarine, and chopped pecans, and cut together like pie crust. Press into 9x13 pan and bake for 12-15 minutes at 350°F. Let cool.

Second layer: Beat cream cheese, Cool Whip, and powdered sugar together until smooth. Spread on first layer.

Third layer: Beat together until thick (about 1 minute) the chocolate pudding mix, vanilla, and milk. Pour over second layer.

Fourth Layer: Put remaining Cool Whip on top. Sprinkle with chopped pecans. *Makes 12 servings.*

PITTER PATTER PEANUT DESSERT

- 1½ cups crushed vanilla wafers
- ¼ cup butter or margarine, melted
- 2 Tbsp plus ½ cup chunky peanut butter
- ½ cup chopped peanuts
- 2 (8 oz) packages cream cheese, softened
- ½ cup sugar
- 2 tsp vanilla
- 4 eggs
- 2 (8 oz) containers frozen whipped topping, thawed
- 1 (11.75 oz) jar hot fudge ice cream topping

Directions:

In a bowl, combine wafers, butter, 2 Tbsp peanut butter, and peanuts. Mix until crumbly. Press one cup of the mixture into the bottom of a 12-cup bundt pan.

In a large bowl, combine cream cheese, sugar, ½ cup peanut butter, and vanilla. Beat 3 minutes at high speed. Beat in eggs one at a time. Fold in whipped topping. Spoon half of the cheese mixture over the crumbs in the pan. By spoonfuls, drop half of the hot fudge; then add remaining cheese mixture. Marble by cutting through with a table knife. Sprinkle with remaining crumbs; freeze until solid.

Remove dessert from freezer 30 minutes before you serve it. Then unmold it onto a serving dish and drizzle with more hot fudge sauce. Sprinkle with peanuts, if desired.

BABY BROWNIE BITES

- 1 brownie mix
- 2 squares white chocolate (baking)
- 2 Tbsp milk
- 1 (8 oz) package cream cheese, soft
- ¼ cup powdered sugar
- 1 cup whipped topping

Directions:

Spray a mini-muffin tin with cooking spray. Prepare the brownie mix according to cake-like directions. Fill each tin ⅔ full. Bake 14 minutes in 325°F oven until the edges are set but not completely done.

Immediately press an indention into cups. Cool and remove from pan. Bake remaining batter.

Microwave the white chocolate and milk for 1 minute. Stir and cool. Combine cream cheese and powdered sugar until blended. Stir in white chocolate mix and blend until smooth. Add whipped topping. Spoon or pipe mixture into the cooled brownie cups.

You can color the filling with pink or blue food coloring to make it more special for a baby shower.

CUDDLY PECAN CUPS

- 1½ sticks butter
- 1 small package cream cheese
- 1 cup flour

Directions:

Cream first two ingredients and then add flour. Make 36 balls and press into small cupcake tins, shaping up along edges like small tart shells.

Filling:

- 2 eggs, beaten
- 1½ cups brown sugar
- 1½ tsp vanilla
- 2 Tbsp butter, melted
- 4 oz pecans, chopped

Directions:

Mix all ingredients and place in lined muffin tins. Bake at 350°F for 15 minutes, then 20 minutes at 250°F. Let cool and remove from tins.

LITTLE LEMON BARS

Crust:

- 2 cups flour
- ½ cups powdered sugar
- 1 cup margarine
- ¼ tsp salt

Directions:

Mix together until crumbly. Press into a 9x13 pan halfway up the sides. Bake crust at 350°F for 12 minutes.

Topping:

- ¼ tsp salt
- Juice of 2 lemons or ⅓ cup reconstituted lemon juice
- 4 eggs
- 3 Tbsp flour
- 2 cups white sugar

Directions:

Mix all together. Pour over crust and bake for 20 minutes at 350°F. Sprinkle immediately with powdered sugar.

BRIDAL SHOWERS

Theme: Celebrating the love between a special couple as they begin their marriage together, with each other and with God.

Verses to share and meditate on:

1 Corinthians 13:13, *And now these three remain: faith, hope and love. But the greatest of these is love.*

Genesis 2:24

Colossians 3:18–19

Ephesians 5:22–23

Ephesians 5:25

Ephesians 5:31

1 Peter 3:7

Love is in the air! What's more heartwarming than seeing two people in love? Especially when they both love God and want to have a home that will honor and glorify Him. As a church family, we are able to support them and share in their joy. To help them establish this new home, we can shower them with our love, blessing, and gifts.

Start with organizing a committee and having a chairperson to be in charge. These are some of the areas you will need to include:

1. Date and Time: Check with honorees for date and time that works good for them. Ask if they would like the shower to be only ladies or if they would like a couple's shower for both of them to attend.

2. Announcement and Invitations: You will need to put details of the shower in the church bulletin and ask the honoree if there is anyone that she might like you to send an invitation to. Ask her to give you a list with addresses. Make sure to do this a few weeks before the event.

3. Gift and Card: Have one person on the committee who will check the bridal registries and purchase the committee gift.

4. Bulletin Boards: If you have a bulletin board in the room where your shower is to be held, be sure to decorate it by having the couple's name or wedding date on it or a verse about love.

5. Decorations: Decorate in the bride's colors or personality. (Example: If she likes music, decorate with musical notes; if she likes gardening, use flowers and seed packets, etc.)

6. Food committee: Find out some of the couple's favorite foods or if there is something they can't eat.

7. Paper Items: Purchase plates, napkins, and cups in the theme colors.

8. Music: Choose a few songs to sing about love, or have soft romantic type music in the background as people arrive.

9. Games and Prizes: Find fun games and prizes you know the honoree with enjoy.

10. Devotional: Ask someone who knows the couple to share some thoughts from God's Word on marriage.

These ideas are taken from *Let's Plan a Party*[4] resource party planning book available through Regular Baptist Press bookstore. It

---

4   Ibid

gives you everything for planning these fellowships. It has theme and decoration ideas, food and recipes, songs, games and prizes to go with the theme, name tags, outlines, and a devotional. The CD included lets you copy the games, assignment sheet, week by week responsibilities, and much more!

RECIPES:

LEMON BLUEBERRY LAYERED DESSERT

- 1 pound cake
- 2 lemons
- 1½ cups milk
- 2 (3.4) packages lemon instant pudding
- 1 (8 oz) sour cream
- 1 (8 oz) whipped topping
- 2 cups blueberries
- 1 square white chocolate

Directions:

Cut or tear pound cake into 1-inch pieces. Zest lemon and set aside. Juice the lemon and sprinkle over cake pieces and toss.

In bowl combine milk, sour cream, half of whipped topping, and lemon zest. Add pudding mix and whisk until smooth and thickened.

In a 9x13 or a glass trifle dish, layer ⅓ cake, ⅓ blueberries, and ⅓ shaved white chocolate. Top with pudding mixture and repeat layers two more times. Top with rest of whipped topping. May add a few blueberries to garnish.

BETTER THAN EVER CHOCOLATE CAKE

- 1 German chocolate cake mix
- 1 (14 oz) can sweetened condensed milk

- 1 (11.75 oz) jar caramel ice cream topping
- 1 (8 oz) container frozen whipped topping, thawed
- 2 Heath candy bars, crushed

Directions:
Prepare cake mix according to directions on box. Bake in a
9x13 pan. Cool. Poke holes in each layer with a small wooden
handle. Mix together sweetened condensed milk and caramel
topping; pour over cake. Spread on whipped topping and
sprinkle with Heath candy bars. Refrigerate.

WEDDING TEA CAKES

- 1 cup margarine
- ½ cup powdered sugar
- 2¼ cups sifted flour
- ¼ tsp salt
- 1 tsp vanilla
- ¾ cup chopped pecans

Directions:
Cut ingredients together with pastry cutter. Chill dough for
1 hour. Shape into small balls or logs. Place on cookie sheet.
Bake at 450°F for 7-10 minutes. Cakes will be brown on the
bottom but not on the top. Roll in powdered sugar. Cool and
roll in powdered sugar again.

COCONUT CREAM CAKE

- ½ cup shortening
- ½ cup margarine
- 2 cups sugar
- 5 eggs, room temperature

- 1 cup buttermilk
- 1 tsp baking soda
- 2 cups flour
- 1 Tbsp vanilla
- 1 ⅔ cups coconut

Frosting:

- ½ cup margarine, softened
- 1 (8 oz) package cream cheese, softened
- 1 lb powdered sugar
- 1 Tbsp vanilla
- 1 cup coconut
- 1 cup chopped nuts

Directions:

For cake, cream shortening, margarine, and sugar. Separate eggs; add yolks to shortening mixture. Combine buttermilk and baking soda. Stir buttermilk and flour, alternately, into egg mixture. Beat egg whites until stiff; add vanilla. Fold into cake mixture. Fold in coconut. Spray and flour three 8" or 9" pans. Bake at 350°F for approximately 30 minutes.

For frosting, cream margarine and cream cheese. Add powdered sugar and vanilla. Fold in coconut and nuts. Frost cake. Sprinkle additional coconut on top.

GRANDMA MARIE'S WEDDING CAKE

- 1 box cake mix
- 1 cup flour
- ¾ cup sugar
- 1 tsp baking powder
- 1 egg white (for white cake) or 1 egg (for chocolate cake)

- ⅔ cup water
- ½ cup oil
- ½ to 1 tsp vanilla
- ½ to 1 tsp almond flavoring (only for white cake)
- 2 Tbsp cocoa (add to dry ingredients for chocolate cake)

Directions:

Follow cake box directions and then add to it the rest of the ingredients according to which flavor of cake you are making. Bake according to box directions.

Cream Frosting:

- ½ cup white vegetable shortening (Crisco™)
- ¼ cup powdered sugar
- 2 tsp vanilla
- ½ cup lukewarm water
- Dash of salt
- Approx. 2 lb powdered sugar
- 1 tsp corn syrup

Directions:

Beat shortening and powdered sugar together. Add vanilla, water, and a dash of salt. Beat together. Add powdered sugar and beat until it is the right consistency to spread. Adding a little corn syrup will help if you are going to be decorating your cake.

FALL KICK OFF

Theme: Start your fall programs off with a fun fellowship to encourage church workers and to promote the activities of the upcoming year.

Verses to share and meditate on:

1 Corinthians 1:9, *God is faithful, who has called you into fellowship with his Son, Jesus Christ our Lord.*

1 John 1:36

Colossians 2:2

1 Thessalonians 5:11

Hebrews 3:13

Hebrews 10:25

Hebrews 6:18

Philippians 2:1

Each fall of the year is a great time to have a promotion kick off for your Sunday school, Wednesday night youth program, and choir as activities in those areas start back up again after a summer break. Use a football theme and plan a big cookout at a local park for the last half of August. You might want to plan your activity as your regular midweek service. Bring in a couple of grills and cook hot dogs and hamburgers. Furnish buns and condiments, table service, and drinks.

Ask the church families to each bring a side dish and a dessert and to dress casual. Also bring lawn chairs and blankets for children to sit on during the church service.

While the meat is cooking, organize a game of touch or flag football according to different ages. Bring old socks to use as flags.

After the meal, bring everyone together by singing choruses with an onward for Christ theme. The pastor may want to have a short devotional, and then you can divide up into different groups of service areas such as Sunday school teachers and workers, choir directors, AWANA or Wednesday night workers and leaders. Talk about your goals and visions for this new school year.

Later, make it a pep rally by having a bonfire with testimony time!

Don't forget the bug spray!

RECIPES:

MISSISSIPPI BEANS

- 1 lb ground beef, browned and drained
- 1 onion chopped
- 1 bell pepper chopped
- ½ cup barbecue sauce
- 2 Tbsp Worcestershire sauce
- 2 Tbsp mustard
- ½ cup brown sugar
- 4 cans pork and beans

Directions:

Sauté onion and bell pepper. Mix with rest of ingredients and with drained beans. Bake at 350°F for 1 hour.

GERMAN POTATO SALAD

- 4 to 6 red potatoes, cut in pieces with skin on
- 1½ lb smoked sausage
- 1 lb bacon, cut up
- 1 onion
- ½ cup brown sugar
- 2 cups sauerkraut
- A little water and vinegar

Directions:

Cook potatoes and drain. Brown bacon and onion together. Spoon off extra grease but leave some for taste. Add brown sugar, water, and vinegar and bring to a boil. Add kraut and sausage. Then add a pinch of baking soda. Put all together and heat until flavors blend. Works well in a slow cooker.

APPLE BARS

- 6 cups apples, peeled and sliced
- 1 cup sugar
- 3 Tbsp flour
- 4 heaping cups flour
- 1 cup butter-flavored Crisco™
- 1 cup lard
- 1 tsp salt
- 1 cup cold milk

Directions:

Mix apples, sugar, and flour together. Set aside. Cut flour, salt, and Crisco together. Add cold milk and form soft dough. Roll out ½ dough in a rectangular shape to fit a large cookie sheet with sides. Fill with apple mixture and dot apples with margarine.

Roll out the remaining ½ dough for a top crust, cutting slits in crust for air to escape, and seal edges. Sprinkle with sugar. Bake at 375°F for 35-45 minutes. *Makes 24 servings.* Drizzle with a glaze of 1-2 cups powdered sugar and 2 Tbsp cold milk.

APPLE SALAD

- 3 apples, unpeeled and diced
- 1 cup white sugar
- 1 egg
- 2 Tbsp flour
- 1½ cups grapes
- 1 can pineapple tidbits
- 1 cup water
- Butter the size of a hickory nut (about 1 Tbsp)
- 2 Tbsp vinegar
- 2 bananas

Directions:

Mix sugar, water, egg, butter, and vinegar in saucepan and boil until thick, stirring all the time. Cool and fold into diced apples, chopped pecans, grapes, marshmallows, pineapple tidbits, and bananas. The apples will not turn dark in this salad.

PUMPKIN CHOCOLATE CHIP MUFFINS

- 1⅔ cups flour
- ¾ cup sugar
- 1 Tbsp pumpkin pie spice
- 1 tsp baking soda
- ¼ tsp baking powder

- ¼ tsp salt
- 2 eggs, beaten
- 1 cup pumpkin
- ½ cup softened margarine
- 1 cup chocolate chips, mini or regular

Directions:
Mix together the eggs, margarine and pumpkin. Add dry ingredients and mix. Add chocolate chips. Fill cupcake tins or papers. Bake in 350°F oven for 20-25 minutes.

Note: Using mini chips in mini-tins works great but the regular size also works well.

PUMPKIN CHEESECAKE

Crust:

- 1½ cup graham cracker crumbs
- 5 Tbsp melted butter
- 1 Tbsp sugar

Directions:
Mix crust and press into bottom and up the sides of a spring form pan. Bake 5 minutes at 350°F.

Filling:

- 3 (8 oz) packages cream cheese
- 1 cup sugar
- 1 tsp vanilla
- 1 cup canned pumpkin
- 3 eggs
- ½ tsp cinnamon

- ¼ tsp nutmeg
- ¼ tsp allspice

Directions:

Combine cream cheese, sugar, and vanilla and mix until smooth. Add eggs, pumpkin, and spices and beat until smooth and creamy. Pour into crust and bake at 350°F for 60-70 minutes or until top turns darker. Remove from oven and let cool. Then refrigerate until thoroughly chilled and remove from pan.

CHRISTMAS IN OCTOBER

Theme: Working together as a church family to learn more about the missionaries your church supports and those missionary's specific needs.

Verses to share and meditate on:

Luke 10:2, *He told them, "The harvest is plentiful, but the workers are few. Ask the Lord of the harvest, therefore, to send out workers into his harvest field."*

John 4:35

Luke 2:7–14

1 Timothy 6:17–18

1 Corinthians 3:6, 8

Isaiah 9:6

Near the beginning of October, set aside a midweek service to honor the missionaries your church supports and the countries they are serving in. Designate this month to bring in Christmas offerings to be sent to all missionaries by the end of October so they might receive it before Christmas.

Plan a carry-in dinner with a church service to follow. If possible, invite a guest speaker or missionary to share on the topic of missions.

A good project for several Sunday school classes or even the junior or senior high youth would be to set up tables displaying information about each missionary and about the country where they are serving. You could also have a sign-up sheet and have different families take a missionary to report about. A family might even find out what foods are served in their missionary's country and try making and bringing that special food to share. Make sure to have a picture of each missionary on their specific table. You could also contact your missionary and find out if there is anything they would like to share on their table, such as a prayer request during this month of October for missions.

Have a box decorated for Christmas on each missionary's table for notes of holiday greetings and encouragement that church members can drop in the box. These notes can be sent with their Christmas offering gifts.

Make October a month to restock your missionary cupboard. Have boxes marked and easily available in different areas of the church building.

RECIPES:

FANNIE MAY CAKE
- ½ cup margarine
- 4 eggs
- 1 tsp vanilla
- 1 cup sugar
- 1 (16 oz) can Hershey's™ syrup
- 1 cup plus 1 Tbsp flour

Directions:

Cream margarine and sugar, add eggs, vanilla, syrup, and flour. Mix. Pour in ungreased 9x13 pan. Bake at 350°F for 30 minutes. Set aside to cool.

1ˢᵗ topping:

- ½ cup margarine
- 2 Tbsp milk
- Green food coloring
- 2 cups powdered sugar
- 1 tsp mint extract

Directions:

Beat margarine, sugar, and milk. Add mint and coloring. Spread over cooled cake, and refrigerate.

2ⁿᵈ topping:

- 6 Tbsp margarine
- 1 cup semi-sweet chocolate chips

Directions:

Melt margarine and chips. Spread over top and refrigerate.

TURTLE BARS

- German chocolate cake mix
- ⅓ cup evaporated milk
- ¾ cup melted butter
- ⅓ cup evaporated milk
- 1½-2 cups chopped pecans
- 1 cup real milk chocolate chips
- 14 oz melted caramels

Directions:

Combine cake mix, evaporated milk, and melted butter. Pour half of batter into greased, floured 9x13 pan. Bake in 350°F oven for 5 minutes. Base will look puffy but doughy. While base is cooling, mix caramel and evaporated milk in double boiler or microwave. Dribble over base. Add chocolate chips and chopped pecans. Drop remaining batter by spoonfuls over top and bake 18-20 minutes. Do not over bake!

ORANGE VELVET COOKIES

- 1 cup butter-flavored Crisco™, or ½ cup shortening plus ½ cup margarine
- ¾ cup sugar
- 2 eggs
- 1 cup cooked, mashed carrots
- 2 cups flour
- 2 tsp baking powder
- ½ tsp salt
- ¾ cup shredded coconut

Directions:

Mix Crisco, sugar, eggs, and carrots. Blend flour, baking powder, and salt into shortening mixture. Mix in coconut. Lightly spray cookie sheet with cooking spray. Bake 8-10 minutes at 400°F. Bake until no imprint remains when lightly touched. Should be lightly browned on the bottom. Frost when cooled.

Frosting:

- 2½ Tbsp soft butter
- 1½ cups powdered sugar

- 1½ Tbsp orange juice
- 2 tsp grated orange rind

Directions:
Mix in small bowl until smooth and creamy.

COOKIE SALAD

- 1½ cups buttermilk
- 1 can mandarin oranges, drained
- 1 small container Cool Whip™
- 1 small package instant vanilla pudding (dry)
- 1 can pineapple tidbits, drained
- ½ package shortbread strip cookies, crumbled

Directions:
Mix first five ingredients and chill. Add cookies just before serving.

STRAWBERRY PRETZEL SALAD

- 2 cups crushed pretzels, ground
- ¾ cup margarine, softened
- 3 Tbsp sugar
- 8 oz cream cheese
- 8 oz Cool Whip™
- 1 large box strawberry Jello™
- 2 cups hot water
- 2 (10 oz) boxes frozen strawberries, thawed

Directions:
Combine pretzels, margarine, and sugar. Press into 9x13 baking pan. Bake at 400°F for 6-8 minutes. Cool. Mix cream cheese with Cool Whip. Spread on top of cooled pretzels. Mix

Jello, water, and strawberries. Spread on top of cream cheese mixture and cool.

CHERRY FLUFF SALAD

- 1 can cherry pie filling
- 1 (14 oz) can sweetened condensed milk
- 1 (20 oz) can crushed pineapple, drained
- 1 (12 oz) container frozen whipped topping, thawed
- Optional: ½ cup chopped pecans, 2-3 bananas, sliced

Directions:

Mix ingredients together and chill.

Celebrating Life with Your Friends

SOME OF LIFE'S MOST MEMORABLE moments are the good times we celebrate with our church friends. Whether it's a Sunday school class party or just a gathering of close friends, it brings happiness and enjoyment to our everyday lives!

TABLE GAME NIGHT

Theme: Showing warm hospitality on a cold winter night.

Verses to share and meditate on:

Romans 12:13, *Share with the Lord's people who are in need.*
Practice hospitality.

1 Peter 4:9

Mark 9:41

Matthew 25:35–36

Matthew 25:40

Hebrews 13:2

Beat the winter blues by having a fun night of playing games with your friends. It is so easy to get "cabin fever" when it is cold and snowy, and this just might be the best cure! When it is cold and snowy on the outside, have a hot potato party to make everyone warm and toasty on the inside.

Start with a hot potato bar. Serve up baked potatoes with different toppers such as chili, cheese, broccoli, onions, ham, bacon bits, and of course butter and sour cream!

Start by having an organized game time where everyone is together. Have a potato broom race where you divide into two teams.

Give each team a broom and a potato. They must sweep their potato to the other end of the room and back and relay onto the next person on their team. First team to finish wins.

Have a game of Hot Potato! Sit in a circle. Someone is in the middle with eyes closed or blindfolded. Start passing the "hot" potato very quickly. When the person in the middle says stop the one who is holding the potato is out, but first gets to take their turn in the middle. The last person to remain in the circle is the winner.

Have a potato peeling contest for the adults.

Have a "Mr. Potato Head" contest with the kids making faces on baking potatoes. Have a time limit set.

After the organized games, break up into table games, making sure there are games for both adults and kids to play. Puzzles are also fun to work on together as a team. See who can get theirs together first!

Everyone who comes could bring snacks to munch on during board game time such as Chex mix, puppy chow, fruit, popcorn, and cookies or bars.

RECIPES :

CHEX™ MIX

- 3 cups Corn Chex cereal
- 3 cups Rice Chex cereal
- 3 cups Wheat Chex cereal
- 1 cup mixed nuts
- 1 cup pecans
- 1 cup dry-roasted peanuts
- 1 cup bite-size pretzels
- 6 Tbsp butter or margarine

- 2 Tbsp Worcestershire sauce
- 1½ tsp seasoned salt
- ¾ tsp garlic powder
- ½ tsp onion powder

Directions:

In large microwavable bowl, mix cereals, nuts, and pretzels; set aside. In small microwavable bowl, microwave butter uncovered on High about 40 seconds or until melted. Stir in seasonings. Pour over cereal mixture; stir until evenly coated. Microwave uncovered on High 5 to 6 minutes, thoroughly stirring every 2 minutes. Spread on paper towels to cool. Store in airtight container.

PEANUT BLOSSOM COOKIES

- 1¾ cups sifted flour
- 1 tsp baking soda
- ½ tsp salt
- ½ cup shortening
- ½ cup peanut butter
- ½ cup sugar
- ½ cup firmly packed brown sugar
- 1 egg
- 2 Tbsp milk
- 1 tsp vanilla
- 48 chocolate stars

Directions:

Sift first three ingredients. Cream together shortening, peanut butter, and sugars. Add 1 unbeaten egg, milk, and vanilla. Beat well. Blend in dry ingredients gradually. Mix thoroughly. Shape into balls. Roll in sugar and place on ungreased cookie sheet. Bake at 350°F for 8 minutes. Remove and place a chocolate star on top. Press down so cookie cracks around edges. Return to oven and bake 2 minutes longer. *Makes 48 cookies.*

FROSTED OATMEAL COOKIES

- 2 cups margarine
- 1 cup sugar
- 1 cup brown sugar
- 2 eggs
- 4 cups flour
- 1 tsp soda
- 3 cups oatmeal

Directions:

Cream margarine, sugar, and eggs. Add flour and soda a little at a time. Mix in oatmeal. Bake on cookie sheet at 325°F for 10-12 minutes.

Frosting:

- ⅓ cup margarine
- 4½ cups powdered sugar
- ⅓ cup evaporated milk
- 1 Tbsp white corn syrup
- 1 tsp vanilla
- ½ cups nuts, if desired

Directions:

Mix together and spread on cookies.

HARRIET'S COOKIES

- 2 sticks margarine
- 2 cups sugar
- 1 cup oil
- 3 eggs
- 2 tsp vanilla
- 5½ cups flour
- 2 tsp baking soda
- 2 tsp cream of tartar

Directions:

Mix all together and chill. Rolls into balls. Bake at 350°F for 10 minutes. Frost.

Frosting:

- 6 Tbsp butter
- 2 tsp vanilla
- 4 Tbsp milk
- ½ tsp salt
- 3½ cups powdered sugar

Directions:

In a medium bowl, beat together. Frost cooled cookies.

FAMILY GYM NIGHT WITH FRIENDS

Theme: Getting together with your friends to work up a sweat and have a fun, fast-paced, rough and rowdy good time.

Verses to share and meditate on:

Psalm 68:3, *But may the righteous be glad and rejoice before God; they be happy and joyful.*

Psalm 144:15

Proverbs 29:18

Proverbs 16:20

Philippians 4:4

Psalm 35:9

Psalm 100:1–2

1 Peter 1:8

John 15:11

Psalm 64:10

Psalm 97:11–12

Isaiah 51:11

What's more fun than a gym filled with activity? In the middle of winter, it provides plenty of room for dads and moms and of course the kids to burn off some energy. (Or moms might just want to sit back and relax!)

See if you can rent a local school gym or YMCA for the evening. Invite your friends and family, or open it up to your Sunday school class.

Make sure to let the kids have their own space to play with balls, jump ropes, ride on scooter boards or just to run for the sake of running!

Adults can organize games of basketball or HORSE. If there is a net, you might set up a game of volleyball.

Have a cool down time with someone sharing some verses on having a joyful, happy heart. Relate it also to the younger kids and all the fun and happy times we can share as God's family.

Have everyone donate some money as they are able and order pizza to share. Bring your own drinks.

RECIPES:

CARAMEL PECAN BARS

Base:

- 1 box yellow cake mix
- ⅓ cup margarine, soft
- 1 egg

Filling:

- 1 (14 oz) can sweetened condensed milk
- 1 egg
- 1 tsp vanilla
- 1 cup chopped pecans
- ½ cup Heath Bits o' Brickle™ chips

Directions:

Preheat oven to 350°F. In large bowl, combine cake mix, margarine, and egg. Mix until crumbly and press in to a 9x13 greased pan. Next mix milk, egg, and vanilla. Stir in nuts and Heath Bits. Pour over base. Bake for 25-35 minutes. Don't overcook. Top will be golden brown but still spongy.

CAN'T LEAVE ALONE BARS

- 1 yellow cake mix
- 2 eggs
- 1 (14 oz) can sweetened condensed milk
- 1 cup chocolate chips
- ¼ cup margarine, cubed

Directions:

Preheat oven to 350°F. Combine dry cake mix, eggs, and oil with floured hands until crumbly. Press ⅔ into a sprayed 9x13 pan. Combine milk, chocolate chips, and butter. Microwave 45 seconds. Stir. Repeat until smooth and pour over the crumble mixture. Drop the rest of the crumble mixture on top of the chocolate by spoonfuls. Bake for 20-25 minutes.

TEXAS BROWNIES

- 2 cups flour
- 2 cups sugar
- ½ cup margarine
- ½ cup Crisco™
- 1 cup strong coffee, or water
- ¼ cup cocoa
- ½ cup buttermilk
- 2 eggs

- 1 tsp vanilla
- 1 tsp baking soda

Frosting:

- 1 stick margarine
- 2 Tbsp cocoa
- 1 tsp vanilla
- ¼ cup milk
- ½ cups powdered sugar

Directions:

Preheat oven to 375°F. Combine flour and sugar. In a separate bowl, combine margarine, shortening, coffee (or water), and cocoa. Stir and heat to boiling. Pour boiling mixture over the flour and sugar. Add buttermilk, eggs, vanilla, and baking soda. Mix well with electric mixer. Pour into a well buttered 11x16 jelly roll pan. Bake for 20 minutes or until done in center.

While brownies bake, prepare the frosting. Combine margarine, cocoa, and milk. Heat to boiling, stirring. Remove from heat and stir in powdered sugar and vanilla until smooth. Pour warm frosting over brownies as soon as you take them out of the oven.

PARTY DESSERT PIZZA

- 1 cup flour
- ½ tsp baking powder
- ½ tsp salt
- ⅛ tsp baking soda
- ½ cup nuts, chopped
- ⅓ cup butter
- 1 cup firmly packed brown sugar

- 1 egg, slightly beaten
- 1 tsp vanilla
- 1 cup chocolate chips

Directions:

Mix flour with baking powder, salt, and soda. Add nuts and set aside. Melt butter and remove from heat. Add sugar and mix well. Cool slightly, then blend in egg and vanilla. Add flour mixture, a small amount at a time, mixing well after each addition. Spread dough in a greased 12-inch pizza pan with 2-inch rim. Sprinkle with chips and bake at 350°F.

CHRISTMAS CAROLING AND SOUP SUPPER

Theme: Spending an afternoon or evening celebrating Christ's birth by singing praises to God and letting our light shine to friends and neighbors.

Verses to share or meditate on:

Isaiah 9:6, *For to us a child is born, to us a son is given, and the government will be on his shoulders. And he will be called Wonderful Counselor, Mighty God, Everlasting Father, Prince of Peace.*

Luke 2:1–20

Ten Popular Christmas Carols:

1. *The First Noel*
2. *Little Town of Bethlehem*
3. *Joy to the World*
4. *Silent Night*
5. *Come All Ye Faithful*
6. *We Three Kings*
7. *Angels We Have Heard on High*
8. *Hark the Herald Angels*

9. *It Came Upon the Midnight Clear*

10. *We Wish You a Merry Christmas*

Christmas is filled with so many good traditions! One of them is to go Christmas caroling. Plan your own caroling outing. Start by getting a group of friends or family or your Sunday school class together for a planning session. It will also be a time of encouragement and blessing to others as you go caroling.

First, decide what homes you would like to stop at. If you carol in town, you may want to walk up the street and stop at homes along the way. If you are in the country, you may want to carpool to each stop. Let the kids sing a few of their favorite songs.

Another option is to go caroling at a nursing home. There you can go up and down the halls and briefly stop at each door. Check with the nursing home to see what time of day would work best for them before you come.

Before your time of caroling, you might want to have some sandwiches and soup. That will make you warm on the inside, so you don't get so cold when you go outside!

Enjoy the lights and sights and sounds of Christmas as you take in the town. The lights on a new blanket of snow remind us that we are to be lights in a dark and sinful world. Shine your light as you sing about the Savior!

Later come back to hot, steamy mugs of hot chocolate and plates of Christmas goodies.

RECIPES:

BAKED POTATO SOUP

- ½ stick butter or margarine
- ¼ cup onion, chopped

- ¼ cup flour
- 1 (14.5 oz) can chicken broth
- 1½ cups evaporated milk
- 2-3 medium baking potatoes, baked or microwaved
- Salt and pepper to taste
- 4 strips bacon, cooked and crumbled
- ½ cup cheddar cheese, shredded
- 3 Tbsp sliced green onion

Directions:

Melt butter. Add onion, cook, stirring occasionally, for 1-2 minutes or until tender. Stir in flour. Gradually stir in broth and evaporated milk. Scoop potato pulp from one potato, mash. Add pulp to broth mixture. Cook over medium heat, stirring occasionally, until mixture just comes to a boil. Dice remaining potato skin and potatoes; add to soup. Heat through. Season with salt and pepper. Top each serving with bacon, cheese, and green onion.

TACO SOUP

- 1 (48 oz) can tomato juice
- 1 can Mexican stewed tomatoes
- 1 lb ground beef, browned and drained
- ¼ cup chopped onion
- 1 can corn
- 1 can pinto beans
- 1 can black beans
- 1 can chili beans
- 1 package taco seasoning
- 1 package ranch dressing mix

- Tortilla chips
- Grated cheddar cheese

Directions:

Combine first ten ingredients in slow cooker and simmer on low 4-6 hours. Serve over crushed tortilla chips. Top with grated cheddar cheese.

RANCH HAND CHILI

- 2 lbs ground beef
- Salt and pepper to taste
- 1 (46 oz) can tomato juice
- 1 package chili seasoning
- 1 cup salsa
- ½ cup brown sugar
- Optional: sour cream, grated cheddar cheese

Directions:

Brown ground beef. Season with salt and pepper. Add tomato juice, seasoning, salsa, and brown sugar. Simmer on the stove for 1 hour or longer (or use a slow cooker). Top with sour cream and grated cheddar cheese.

CHICKEN AND RICE SOUP

- ½ cup butter
- 1 chopped onion
- ½ cup chopped celery
- ½ cup chopped carrots
- ½ lb fresh mushrooms, sliced
- ¾ cup flour
- 6 cups chicken broth

- 2 cups wild rice (Uncle Ben's™)
- 1 lb cooked chicken breast
- ½ tsp salt
- ½ tsp curry powder
- ½ tsp dry mustard
- Pepper to taste
- ½ cup slivered almonds
- 2 cups half-and-half

Directions:

Brown vegetables in butter. Add flour, stir, and then pour in broth. Add remaining ingredients except for half-and-half. Add it after other ingredients are warm.

EASY POTATO-SAUSAGE SOUP

- ½ lb ground pork sausage
- 16 oz frozen shredded hash browns
- 1 large onion, chopped
- 1 can chicken broth
- 1-2 cups water
- 1 can cream of celery soup
- 1 can cream of chicken soup
- 2 cups milk

Directions:

Brown sausage, stirring to crumble. Drain fat and rinse sausage. Return to dutch oven or slow cooker. Add potatoes, onion, chicken broth, and water. Bring to boil. Cover, reduce heat, and simmer 30 minutes. Add soups and milk. Cook, stirring often, until thoroughly blended (heated). *Makes 8 servings.*

BEEF AND MUSHROOM BARLEY SOUP

- 1½ lb boneless beef chuck, cut into ¾-inch cubes
- 1 Tbsp oil
- 1 lb fresh mushrooms, sliced
- 1 tsp salt
- ½ tsp pepper
- 1 tsp thyme
- 2 cups onion, finely chopped
- 1 cup carrots, diced
- ½ cup celery, sliced
- 2 garlic cloves, minced
- 1 can beef broth
- 1 can chicken broth
- ½ cup medium pearl barley
- 2 cups water
- 3 Tbsp fresh parsley, chopped

Directions:

In a dutch oven, brown meat in oil. Remove meat with a slotted spoon and set aside. Sauté onion, carrots, and celery in drippings over medium heat until tender, about 5 minutes. Add mushrooms, garlic, and thyme; cook and stir for 3 minutes. Add broths, water, barley, salt and pepper. Return meat to pan; bring to boil. Reduce heat; cover and simmer for 1-2 hours or until barley and meat are tender. Add parsley.

MYSTERY DINNER

Theme: It's a mystery. This will challenge your friends or church group as you are given clues about your dinner and you have to decide what the best choices to order are for each stage of your dinner. Later, your choices will be revealed to you. God had a mystery that He revealed to the prophets and apostles through the leading of the Holy Spirit. Through faith in Jesus Christ, God would allow the Jews and Gentiles alike to be saved.

Verses to share and meditate on:

1 Corinthians 2:7, *No, we declare God's wisdom, a mystery that has been hidden and that God destined for our glory before time began.*

1 Corinthians 15:51

Ephesians 1:9

Ephesians 5:32

Colossians 1:26

1 Timothy 3:16

Matthew 4:11

Mark 4:11

As people arrive, attach name tags of famous people on the back of your guests. They will need to ask each other questions about who they are. Questions may be something like "Am I a singer?" "Am I a girl?" Answers can only be "yes" or "no." This is a good ice-breaker.

Plan a mystery dinner for your guests by having a menu printed like the one below. Each person picks five numbers at a time, and those five items are served and then taken away. They then get to pick five more, which are served and taken away. This is repeated until all twenty items have been served. It will be interesting and fun to see what they order, because their utensils and drinks are included on the menu. They may have to eat their dessert with a carrot stick!

Menu: (Includes main course, utensils, drinks and dessert)

1. Old Glory
2. A Taste of Europe
3. Cow Chip
4. Bloodshot Eyes
5. Farmer's Helper
6. Markers and Glue
7. Honeymooner's Prayer
8. Muddy River
9. Gooey Canoes
10. Lover's Delight
11. Chip Off the Old Block
12. Polly's Delight
13. Gangster's Friend
14. Staff of Life
15. Niagara Falls
16. Sleepy Relative

17. Green Daggers

18. Cold Cow

19. Eden's Temptation

20. Tall, Dark, and Handsome

Your guests are served the following according to the numbers they have chosen. They get five items at a time.

Real Menu:

1. Lasagna

2. Italian Dressing

3. Butter

4. Olives

5. Fork

6. Carrots with Ranch Dressing

7. Lettuce (alone)

8. Coffee

9. Celery with Peanut Butter

10. Spoon

11. Toothpick

12. Crackers

13. 1 Knife

14. Bread Stick

15. Water

16. Napkin

17. Pickle Spear

18. Ice Cream

19. Fruit Salad

20. Chocolate Cake

After dinner is finished, play a version of the old TV show called "What's My Line?" Select a panel of four or five and put blindfolds on them. Select a person to be the mystery guest. They should have a name tag so everyone there knows who the mystery guest is pretending to be.

Each person on the panel gets to ask ten questions, which can only be answered by "yes" or "no" by the mystery guest. If the person asking the question gets a "no," then they must let the next person have a turn to ask questions.

Whenever a panel member thinks they can identify the mystery guest, they can ask the question "Are you _____?" If the answer is yes, they are the winner!

RECIPES:

LASAGNA

- 1 (16 oz) package lasagna noodles, cooked and drained
- 2 (26 oz each) jars spaghetti sauce
- 1 lb ground beef, cooked and drained
- 1 (8 oz) carton cottage cheese
- 6-8 cups shredded mozzarella cheese

Directions:

Add ground beef to spaghetti sauce. In a 9x13 pan, start with sauce on the bottom. Then layer the noodles, cottage cheese, sauce, and mozzarella cheese twice, ending with mozzarella cheese on top. Bake at 350°F for 40-50 minutes.

FRUIT SALAD

Combine different fruits such as fresh strawberries, blueberries, grapes, mandarin oranges, bananas, pineapple chunks, etc. Add a can of peach pie filling and stir to cover fruit.

CREAMY FRUIT SALAD

- 1 (11 oz) can mandarin oranges, drained
- 1 (84 oz) can sliced peaches, drained
- 1 (8 oz) can pineapple chunks, drained
- 1 cup miniature marshmallows
- 4 oz cream cheese, softened
- ½ cup plain (or vanilla) yogurt
- ¼ cup sugar (sugar is not needed with vanilla yogurt)

Directions:

Combine oranges, peaches, pineapple, and marshmallows. In a small bowl, beat the cream cheese, yogurt and sugar until smooth; pour over fruit and toss to coat. Refrigerate for 15 minutes. *Makes 4 servings.*

CHOCOLATE CAKE

- 1 package devil's food cake mix
- 1¼ cups water
- 3 eggs
- ⅓ cup vegetable oil
- 1 (12 oz) jar raspberry jam
- 1 can chocolate frosting
- Sliced almonds

Directions:

Grease and flour 3 round cake pans. In a large bowl, combine cake mix, water, eggs, and oil. Beat at low speed 30 seconds, and medium speed 2 minutes. Pour into prepared pans. Bake at 350°F for 15-18 minutes. Cool in pans 5 minutes. Turn onto cooling racks until completely cool.

Melt jam in saucepan over medium heat. Place one cake on serving plate. Brush a thin layer of jam over cake and spread frosting over jam. Repeat with second layer. Place third layer on top. Spread sides with remaining frosting. Bring frosting up around edge of cake to form a small ridge. Spread remaining jam over top of cake. Garnish with almond slices. *Makes 15 servings.*

LET'S GO BOWLING!

Theme: Trusting God to be our faithful and solid rock.

Verses to share and meditate on:

Lamentations 3:22–23, *Because of the Lord's great love we are not consumed, for his compassions never fail. They are new every morning; great is your faithfulness.*

2 Samuel 22:2, 47

Psalm 27:5

Psalm 61:2

Psalm 31:3

Deuteronomy 7:9

Psalm 119:89–90

Numbers 23:19

2 Peter 3:9

Isaiah 46:11

Isaiah 54:10

Psalm 105:8

Are you ready for some fun and excitement? Let's go bowling! Plan an evening to rent some lanes at a local bowling alley. Invite a group of friends or your Sunday school class to get together for a bowling bash! You can rent bowling balls and shoes at the bowling alley. Set up four teams (or however many you need) by drawing numbers. Lane #1 will be the highest lane consisting of the people who drew the number 1. Lane #2 will be the 2's and so on. Keep individual scores. The two people on each team with the highest score after a set number of games will move up to the next lane. Unfortunately, the losers in the high lane will have to go clear down to the bottom lane and work their way back up.

See who can remain in the #1 high lane the longest. They will be the solid rock of the evening if they can hold on firm to their spot!

Have fun prizes for each lane when the bowling is all done.

Prizes are things that are round like a bowling ball.

Lane 1: Each player gets a bag of cheese balls.

Lane 2: Each player gets an orange.

Lane 3: The team gets a carton of chocolate-covered malted milk balls to share.

Lane 4: Each player gets a gumball!

Make sure the bowling is all done in fun, especially if you include children.

RECIPES:

SLOPPY JOES

- 3 lb ground beef
- ¼ tsp pepper
- 1 tsp salt
- 2 Tbsp brown sugar
- 1 cup ketchup
- 2 Tbsp lemon juice

- 2 Tbsp vinegar
- ¾ cup water

Directions:

Brown ground beef and drain. Mix together and simmer until it thickens.

HEARTY POTATO CASSEROLE

- 1 (32 oz) bag frozen hash browns
- 1 (16 oz) sour cream
- 1 can cream of chicken soup
- 1 stick margarine
- 8-12 oz shredded colby cheese
- 1 small onion, chopped

Directions:

Mix ingredients together and bake at 350°F for 1-1½ hours.

PARTY POTATOES

- 8-10 potatoes
- Small carton sour cream
- 8 oz cream cheese
- Butter
- Garlic salt
- Salt and pepper to taste
- Chives

Directions:

Boil and mash potatoes. Add the rest of the ingredients. Mix until creamy. Put in baking dish and dot with butter and paprika. Bake 30 minutes at 350°F.

QUICK BACON BROCCOLI RAISIN SALAD

- 16 oz bite-size pieces fresh broccoli
- ½ cup raisins
- ⅓ cup bacon bits
- ¼ cup sunflower seeds
- 8 oz bottle coleslaw dressing

Directions:

Combine and refrigerate 30 minutes. *Makes 4-6 servings.*

ORIENTAL SALAD

- 2 Tbsp vegetable oil
- 3 Tbsp white wine vinegar
- 2 Tbsp white sugar
- 1 (3 oz) package chicken-flavored ramen noodles, crushed (seasoning packet reserved)
- ½ tsp salt
- ½ tsp ground black pepper
- 2 Tbsp sesame seeds
- ¼ cup sliced almonds
- ½ medium head cabbage, shredded (or bag already prepared)
- 5 green onions, chopped

Directions:

Preheat oven to 350°F. In a medium bowl, whisk together the oil, vinegar, sugar, ramen noodle spice mix, salt, and pepper to create a dressing.

Place sesame seeds and almonds in a single layer on a medium baking sheet. Bake in the preheated oven 10 minutes, or until lightly brown.

In a large salad bowl, combine the cabbage, green onions, and crushed ramen noodles. Pour dressing over the cabbage, and toss to coat evenly. Top with toasted sesame seeds and almonds.

SOFTBALL CHALLENGE

Theme: Live a successful Christian life. There will always be challenges to face in life, but we can overcome them and be successful when we trust in Christ. Hopefully then the people that come after us will see we have lived faithful, God-honoring lives.

Verses to share and meditate on:

Joshua 1:8-9, *Keep this Book of the Law always on your lips; meditate on it day and night, so that you may be careful to do everything written in it. Then you will be prosperous and successful. Have I not commanded you? Be strong and courageous. Do not be afraid; do not be discouraged, for the Lord your God will be with you wherever you go.*

Ecclesiastes 10:10

Philippians 4:13

Psalm 1:1-3

Genesis 39:2–3

Psalm 122:6

Deuteronomy 5:32–33

Plan an afternoon or summer evening to play some softball! Locate a ball field in your area that is not being used, or contact a little league or ball field at your local school and ask if there would be a field available on the day of your activity and reserve it for your group.

Plan to have a barbecue/picnic with hot dogs and brats. Ask everyone to bring their own meat to grill. You may want to have families bring cookies or bars and chips to share. Big coolers of drinks such as lemonade or iced tea could be provided as well as paper plates and cups. You will probably have to bring in a charcoal grill and have it fired up ahead of time. Provide wet wipes or a cooler of water for softball players to wash up with before they eat!

Plan when game time will start. Make sure to start with singing the national anthem, and also ask one of the men to pray for the food and for safety for the game. Then . . . play ball!!!

Put the meat on the grill so those who aren't playing can go ahead and eat as they watch the game.

Remind people to bring lawn chairs and blankets to sit on as you cheer on the ball players and enjoy a great summer evening together with your friends.

RECIPES:

POTATO SALAD

- 10 white potatoes (boiled with skins on until soft but not mushy)
- 6 hard-boiled eggs, peeled and chopped
- ¼ cup white onion, chopped
- 1 cup hamburger relish
- 1½ pound Velveeta™ cheese, chopped
- ¼ cup sugar
- 1 tsp salt

- ½ tsp pepper
- ½ cup Miracle Whip™ salad dressing
- 1 Tbsp mustard

Directions:

Cool potatoes in cold water, then peel and cut into small chunks. Mix all ingredients and chill.

BAKED BEANS

- 2 (15.5 oz) cans pork and beans, drained
- 1 cup ketchup
- 1½ cup brown sugar
- ¼ cup chopped onion
- 2 Tbsp prepared mustard
- ½ cup mild molasses

Directions:

Preheat oven to 350°F. Stir ingredients together and bake uncovered for 50-60 minutes.

APPLE PIE IN A BAG

Crust:

- 1 cup flour
- ½ tsp salt
- ⅓ cup lard
- 2 Tbsp cold water

Directions:

Cut flour, salt, and lard together until crumbly. Add water and form into ball. Roll out to form a circle crust for bottom of pie tin.

Filling:

- 5 cups apples, peeled, sliced
- 1 cup sugar
- ¼ tsp cinnamon
- ¼ tsp nutmeg
- 1 tsp lemon juice

Directions:

Mix together and put in crust.

Topping:

- ½ cup butter, soft
- 1 cup flour
- 1 cup sugar

Directions:

Cut together and put on top of apple filling. Sprinkle with a little more cinnamon and nutmeg on the top. Place in a brown paper bag and fold over the open edge. Place on a cookie sheet and bake in a 400°F oven for 1 hour.

4TH OF JULY PICNIC

Theme: Celebrating our freedoms in America with friends and family under God's big, blue, summer sky. Remember our true freedom is in Christ. Enjoy a relaxing summertime day.

Verses to share and meditate on:

Matthew 11:28–29, *Come to me, all you who are weary and burdened, and I will give you rest. Take my yoke upon you and learn from me, for I am gentle and humble in heart, and you will find rest for your souls.*

Isaiah 14:7

Hebrews 4:9

Exodus 31:15

Psalm 23:1–3

Psalm 16:9

Psalm 37:7

John 8:38

Galatians 5:1

Romans 6:18

To celebrate the 4th of July with some good friends and family, plan a picnic! Start your day by going to your town's 4th of July parade, if there is one. Many small towns in the USA have a parade to celebrate our independence.

After the parade, plan to have everyone meet at a park, your church lawn, or someone's home. Have a potluck meal or plan to bring a grill and have everyone bring meat to cook on the grill and a couple of side dishes.

If the time is right for sweet corn, make sure to include a sweet corn feast with sticks of butter to roll it in. What a great way to enjoy a summertime treat!

Bring lawn chairs and blankets to relax on. Plan organized games for the kids such as hopscotch on the sidewalk, 3-legged races, red rover, dodgeball, or volleyball for the adults. If the day is nice and hot, turn on the sprinkler for the kids to run through! Maybe even a few adults will want to cool off too!

Later in the afternoon, bring out cold watermelons that have been chilling in ice water. Slice into wedges and eat outside so you can have a seed-spitting contest.

Don't hurry home! Bask in the warmth of the sun. Take the day slow and relax. Enjoy your friends' good company. Relish sitting under a big old shade tree and enjoy God's creation. The wide open spaces around you will make you feel free indeed!

RECIPES:

FRESH SWEET CORN

- 4 quarts cut corn
- ½ cup sugar
- 4 tsp salt
- 1 quart water

Directions:

Mix well. Boil 5-7 minutes. Stir constantly while cooking. Cool and eat or put in freezer bags and freeze.

PICKLED RIGATONI

- 1 large package Rigatoni or pasta of your choice
- 2 Tbsp olive oil
- 1 cup chopped green pepper
- ½ cup chopped onion
- 1 large jar pimentos or 1 red bell pepper, chopped
- ½ tsp parsley flakes
- 10-12 cherry tomatoes, sliced in half
- 1 cup mini pepperoni
- ½ cup feta cheese
- ¼ cup sliced olives, if desired

Dressing:

- 1½ cups vinegar
- 1½ cups sugar
- 1 tsp salt
- 2 tsp pepper
- 2 Tbsp mustard
- 1 pinch garlic powder
- 1 pinch Accent (flavor enhancer)

Directions:

Cook rigatoni until it is at chewy stage, not overdone. Rinse, drain, and cool. Heat vinegar and sugar to just below boiling. Add salt and pepper. Cool slightly. Add oil, green pepper, onion, pimentos, and rigatoni. Refrigerate for several hours. Keeps for 2 weeks in the refrigerator.

SPINACH SALAD

- 8 cups spinach
- 1 cup sliced mushrooms
- 4 boiled eggs
- 1 cup shredded Swiss cheese
- ⅓ cup black olives
- 6 slices bacon chopped

Dressing:

- 1 cup olive oil
- ½ cup sugar
- ¼ cup vinegar
- ⅓ cup ketchup
- ¼ tsp garlic powder

Directions:

Mix salad together in a large bowl. Pour dressing on salad, mix and toss.

TACO SALAD

- 1 lb ground beef
- 1 package taco seasoning mix
- 1 can red kidney beans, rinsed and drained
- 1 small-medium onion, chopped
- 2 cups shredded cheddar cheese
- 3-4 tomatoes, chopped
- 1 head lettuce, shredded
- 1 bag Dorito™ chips, crushed
- 1 (8 oz) bottle fat-free Western™ salad dressing

Directions:

Brown ground beef and taco mix together. In large bowl, stir together seasoned meat, beans, onion, cheese, and tomatoes. Refrigerate overnight. Just before serving, stir in lettuce, chips, and salad dressing. *Makes 20 servings.*

SPINACH MANDARIN SALAD WITH
SWEET FRENCH DRESSING

- 2 lb raw spinach, washed, dried, torn
- ¾ cup chopped walnuts
- 1 small onion, chopped
- 4 oz can mandarin oranges, drained
- 1 cup shredded cheddar cheese
- 6 slices bacon, fried and crumbled

Directions:

Toss together all but last ingredient. Add dressing and bacon just before serving.

SWEET FRENCH DRESSING

- 1 cup Crisco™ oil
- ½ cup ketchup
- ½ cup sugar
- ¼ cup vinegar
- 1 tsp Worcestershire sauce

Directions:

Mix dressing ingredients together. Pour over salad just before serving.

CRAB SALAD

- 1 large package imitation crab
- 2 cups cooked bow tie pasta
- ¾ cup diced celery
- 10-12 cherry tomatoes, cut in half
- Black olives, sliced
- Ranch salad dressing to taste

Directions:
Combine all ingredients and chill.

CAMPOUT

Theme: Take a weekend to enjoy the glories and the wonder of God's great outdoors! As you sit around the campfire, talk about how God used fire and smoke at different times to show His power and glory.

Verses to share and meditate on:

Psalm 104:1–4, *Praise the Lord, my soul. Lord my God, you are very great; you are clothed with splendor and majesty. The Lord wraps himself in light as with a garment; he stretches out the heavens like a tent and lays the beams of his upper chambers on their waters. He makes the clouds his chariots and rides on the wings of the wind. He makes winds his messengers, flames of fire his servants.*

Hebrews 12:29

Exodus 24:17

Exodus 13:22

1 Kings 18:38

Hebrews 12:29

Psalm 97:1–6

Organize a few families or an entire adult Sunday school class to go camping over the weekend. Fall is a wonderful time to enjoy the outdoors when the leaves on the trees are changing and turning colors and the air at night is cool and crisp.

Reserve a campground for your tents and campers. Or if you know someone with a timber or pasture, you might want to be all by yourselves and just rough it! Packing up is a lot of work, but it is worth it. Set up camp and get a good fire going to cook over. If you have a fire ring with a grate, that will make cooking much easier, especially if you choose to use a big cooking pot to cook chili or stew. There is nothing better than slow-cooked soup on an open fire. Just be sure to stir it often! Have everyone furnish salads, crackers, breads, desserts, and drink.

While the food is cooking, plan on enjoying some activities as families. If you have an open area and the wind is right, try kite flying. You could collect rocks to put around the fire.

Be sure to use your campfire for s'mores later in the evening. Marshmallows cooked on a stick and then squished between chocolate and graham crackers are a great treat!

Be sure to spend time sitting around the fire. Talk about times in the Bible that God used fire to show Himself mighty. Sing songs and tell funny stories. See who can identify constellations or just teach the little ones how to find the Big Dipper. Maybe some will even choose to sleep under the stars! If your church has a projector and someone who is techy, then maybe you could watch a movie outside using a bed sheet and some PVC pipes for the movie screen.

Rise and shine the next morning and get the fire stoked to cook breakfast on the grate. A big cookie sheet works great for frying bacon and eggs, or aluminum foil spread over the grate works as well.

Serve with sweet rolls and milk or juice. Remember to bring paper plates and cups so clean up is easy.

Ask someone to bring an early morning devotional about the glories of God's creation. Enjoy time surrounded by nature with good friends and family!

RECIPES:

FIVE-HOUR OVEN STEW

- 3 lb stew meat
- 6 carrots, chopped
- ½ cup celery, chopped
- 5 large potatoes, chunked
- 1 large onion, diced
- 1 large can V-8™ or tomato juice
- 1 can Italian recipe tomatoes
- 1 can beef broth
- 1 package frozen corn
- 1 tsp salt and pepper
- 2 Tbsp tapioca
- 1 Tbsp sugar

Directions:

Place all ingredients in large roasting pan or slow cooker. Bake tightly covered 275°F for 5 hours or 325°F for 4 hours. If camping, put in a cast iron or heavy dutch oven and set over the campfire.

BEEF JERKY

- 4-5 lb thinly sliced beef
- 4 Tbsp soy sauce

- 4 Tbsp Worcestershire sauce
- 1 Tbsp salsa
- ½ Tbsp ginger
- 2 cloves garlic or 4 tsp garlic salt
- ¼ tsp black pepper
- ½ tsp salt

Directions:

Mix ingredients in bowl. Pour over meat and marinate 4-6 hours or overnight. Put in dehydrator and cook until dry.

GRANDMA'S SWEET ROLLS

- 2 package quick-rise yeast
- ¼ cup sugar
- ½ cup warm water
- 2 eggs
- 1¾ cup lukewarm milk
- 6-6½ cups of flour
- 3 tsp salt
- ¼ cup margarine

Directions:

Mix yeast, sugar, and warm water in small bowl and set aside. In a large bowl beat eggs and lukewarm milk. Add the yeast mixture. Stir in flour, salt, and margarine. Kneed and put into a greased bowl. Let rise until doubled. Roll out on floured surface ¼ to ½ inch thick.

- ¼ cup margarine
- ⅔ cup brown sugar
- White sugar

- Cinnamon
- ½ cup grape jelly

Directions:

Melt margarine and spread out on the dough. Sprinkle with brown sugar and enough white sugar to cover. Sprinkle with cinnamon. Roll up and cut. Place in buttered pan. Let set 15 minutes before baking. Bake at 375°F for 18-20 minutes. Ice rolls by spreading ¼ to ½ cup grape jelly across the top of them.

HOBO HAMBURGER TIN-FOIL DINNER

- ⅓ lb lean ground beef made into fat patty
- 1-2 thick onion slices
- 1 medium potato, sliced
- 1 whole carrot, sliced
- 1 tsp Worcestershire sauce, more or less to taste
- Salt & pepper – generous, but to taste
- 1 Tbsp butter or margarine

Directions:

Start with a layer of onions, then the hamburger, followed by the sliced potatoes, and then the sliced carrots. Add the Worcestershire sauce, and top with salt & pepper (seasoned to taste), and butter.

Note: Other vegetables can be added like corn, peas, sweet peppers, or green beans.

THE ULTIMATE S'MORE

- Vegetable oil
- Graham crackers

- 4 bars (3.5 oz each) dark chocolate with almonds (such as Lindt™), each broken into 3 pieces
- Marshmallows

Directions:

Fold 12 sheets of foil, each 12x20 in., in half crosswise; then oil tops. Center 1 graham cracker on each oiled doubled sheet, then top with a chocolate piece, marshmallow, and another cracker. Gently fold foil over s'mores and crimp to seal.

Heat packets on a cooking grate over glowing coals in a campfire or on a grill over medium heat (about 350°F), turning often just until chocolate softens, 2 to 3 minutes. Or, using tongs, grasp packets on sides and heat over a low fire.

ICE CREAM AND PIE SOCIAL

Theme: God's Promised Land was a land filled with milk (ice cream) and honey (something sweet like pie)! He delights in giving us good things to enjoy. His Word is sweet to taste, and He is good to those who trust in Him!

Verses to share and meditate on:

Exodus 3:8, *So I have come down to rescue them from the hand of the Egyptians and to bring them up out of that land into a good and spacious land, a land flowing with milk and honey.*

Numbers 13:27

Deuteronomy 6:3

Joshua 5:6

Jeremiah 11:5

Ezekiel 20:6

Psalm 37:3–5

Psalm 119:16

Psalm 1:2

There is nothing more delightful on a warm summer evening than a hand-cranked freezer of homemade ice cream and a freshly baked fruit pie! You won't have to invite anyone . . . they will just start coming!

Set a date for everyone to get together and ask them to bring a pie or the ingredients for a freezer of ice cream that will be made while you are all together. Ask the men to be in charge of the ice, salt, and the cranking! They can visit outside under a shade tree as they take turns turning the handle.

An extra treat would be homemade fudge topping that someone who prefers not to make a pie could bring instead.

When the ice cream is done, scoop it into bowls and watch for smiles as everyone enjoys each cool, creamy spoonful!!

Delight in your pie and ice cream, in each other's company, and also delight in the Lord your God and His great love.

RECIPES:

HOMEMADE ICE CREAM

- 4 eggs
- 2 cups sugar
- 2 Tbsp vanilla
- ½ tsp salt
- 1 quart half-and-half
- 1 pint whipping cream

Directions:

Beat eggs and sugar with mixer until creamy. Add remaining ingredients and put in ice cream maker container and then fill with whole milk to designated line on container. Use ice cream maker as directed.

FRESH PEACH PIE

- 1 heaping cup flour
- ¼ cup cold milk

- ½ tsp salt
- ½ cup butter Crisco™
- 8-9 fresh peaches, peeled and sliced, coated with lemon juice or Fruit Fresh™
- 3 Tbsp flour or 3 Tbsp tapioca
- 1 large cup sugar
- ¼ tsp cinnamon

Directions:

Preheat oven to 375°F. Cut flour, salt, and Crisco together until crumbly. Stir in cold milk until dough comes together in a ball. It might be a little sticky but will firm up when you roll out with flour. Roll on floured surface and put in a 9-inch pie pan. Makes 2 crusts. Stir together remaining ingredients. Cook on stove (or in microwave) until thickened, about 6 to 8 minutes. Stir constantly. Remove from heat and pour into bottom crust. Dot with margarine. Add top crust (with a slit in top to let out air). Seal edges. Sprinkle crust with sugar. Bake for 30-35 minutes. *Serves 8*.

TRIPLE BERRY PIE

- 2 unbaked pie crusts
- 1 cup blackberries
- 1 cup red raspberries
- 2 cups blueberries
- 1 cup sugar
- 3 Tbsp cornstarch
- ½ cup water
- 2 Tbsp lemon juice

Directions:

Preheat oven to 350°F. Mix together sugar, cornstarch, and water in medium saucepan. Add berries and lemon juice. Cook on medium heat for 5-7 minutes. Fill pie shell with berry mixture and put on top crust. Brush top with milk and sprinkle with sugar. Bake for 45 minutes. *Serves 8.*

CHERRY PIE

- 3 cups (overflowing) tart red cherries
- 1½ cups sugar
- 3 Tbsp tapioca
- Dash of salt
- 1 tsp almond extract
- 1 Tbsp margarine
- 9-inch pie shells, top and bottom (unbaked)

Directions:

Preheat oven to 375°F. In a saucepan, mix together ingredients. Let set 15 minutes to soften tapioca. Cook until thick, stirring constantly. Pour into pie shell. Dot with margarine. Add top crust. Seal and sprinkle with sugar. Bake for 35-45 minutes. *Serves 8.*

STRAWBERRY-RHUBARB PIE

- 1 cup strawberries
- 2 cups rhubarb
- 3 Tbsp flour
- 1 cup sugar (overflowing)
- ½ tsp cinnamon
- 9-inch pie shell for top and bottom

Directions:

Preheat oven to 375°F. In a saucepan, stir together ingredients. Cook until thick, stirring constantly. If using fresh fruit, add a little water. Pour into unbaked pie shell. Dot with margarine. Add top crust, seal and sprinkle with sugar. Bake for 35-40 minutes. *Serves 8.*

APPLE PIE

- 1 heaping cup flour
- ¼ cup cold milk
- ½ tsp salt
- ½ cups butter Crisco™
- 6-7 tart baking apples (Jonathan, Winesap, Granny Smith), peeled and sliced
- 1 cup sugar
- 1 tsp cinnamon
- 3 Tbsp flour
- 2 Tbsp butter or margarine

Directions:

Preheat oven to 375°F. Cut flour, salt, and Crisco together until crumbly. Stir in cold milk until dough comes together in a ball. It might be a little sticky, but will firm up when you roll out with flour. Roll on floured surface and put in a 9-inch pie pan. Make 2 crusts. Stir apples, sugar, cinnamon, and flour together and pour in pie crust. Dot with 2 Tbsp butter or margarine. Add top crust, seal, and sprinkle with sugar. Bake for 45-60 minutes or until bubbly in center. *Makes 8 servings.*

CHOCOLATE SILK PIE

- 2 sticks butter
- 2 cups powdered sugar
- 2 squares unsweetened chocolate
- 1 tsp vanilla
- 2 eggs
- 1 prepared 9-inch pie crust
- Cool Whip™

Directions:

Cream butter, adding powdered sugar gradually. Melt chocolate in microwave. When cool, add to butter mixture along with vanilla. Add eggs, one at a time, beating at high speed for 4 minutes after each egg. Do not overbeat or butter may tend to melt. Refrigerate at least 2 hours. Cover pie with Cool Whip. Garnish with shaved chocolate. *Serves 8.*

BANANA CREAM PIE

- ¾ cup sugar
- 3 Tbsp cornstarch
- ¼ tsp salt
- 1 tsp vanilla
- 2 cups milk (partly cream)
- 3 egg yolks, slightly beaten
- 2 Tbsp butter
- 2-3 bananas
- 16 oz Cool Whip
- 1 graham cracker pie crust

Directions:

Combine first 7 ingredients together in saucepan and cook on low to medium heat, stirring constantly until smooth, creamy, and thick. Cut bananas into slices and put on bottom of pie crust. Pour hot pudding over top of bananas. Place plastic wrap over surface and put in refrigerator until set (2-3 hours). Top with Cool Whip. *Serves 8.*

BOUNTIFUL HARVEST DINNER

Theme: Showing our thankfulness to God for all He has done and provided for us. Doing what we can to provide for others with a Thanksgiving style dinner.

Verses to share and meditate on:

Psalm 100:1–5, *Shout for joy to the Lord, all the earth. Worship the Lord with gladness; come before him with joyful songs. Know that the Lord is God. It is he who made us, and we are his; we are his people, the sheep of his pasture. Enter his gates with thanksgiving and his courts with praise; give thanks to him and praise his name. For the Lord is good and his love endures forever; his faithfulness continues through all generations.*

Psalm 92:1

Psalm 107:1

1 Thessalonians 5:18

Psalm 95:2

We have so much to be thankful for as Christians. We have a God who loves us and has provided a way for us to have a home in heaven through Jesus Christ. When we place our trust in Him, we receive eternal life. We enjoy the freedom to worship God here in America.

We also have warm homes to live in and an abundance of food to eat at our tables. Because God has so richly blessed us, we should be willing and able to bless others.

Start by finding some families who would like to help with planning a Thanksgiving-type meal for some elderly or needy people in your church or neighborhood. It would probably be best to plan your dinner the weekend before Thanksgiving.

Assign each participating family a portion of the meal to prepare at their home.

Roast turkey(s) and gravy from the turkey juices

Slow cookers of a vegetable such as corn or green beans

Slow cookers of mashed potatoes

Slow cookers of dressing

Bread or rolls

Jello salad

Pumpkin pie

Have everyone bring their prepared food to the church or one of the homes and make an assembly line to fill the containers. Purchase large carry-out containers for the turkey, dressing, potatoes and gravy, and vegetable. Purchase small carry-out containers for the jello and pumpkin pie. The rolls can be put in Zip-lock™ bags to stay fresh. Put each meal into a grocery bag and label who it is to be delivered to and who it is from. You might also want to print out Psalm 100 and attach it to one of the containers.

Assign volunteers to take the meals to intended recipients. Contact families ahead of time so they will know someone is coming. Be sure volunteers know to spend a few minutes visiting with each recipients of a Thanksgiving meal. Everyone involved will receive a blessing!

RECIPES:

SCALLOPED CORN

- 1 can creamed corn
- 1 can whole kernel corn with juice
- 1 stick butter or margarine
- 1 egg, beaten
- ½ cup sour cream
- 1 box Jiffy™ corn muffin mix
- ½ cup green onion, chopped

Directions:

Mix ingredients together and put in baking dish that has been sprayed with Pam. Bake 45-50 minutes at 350°F. Transfer to a slow cooker to keep warm.

STUFFING

- 4 cups chicken broth (add milk if you need more liquid)
- ½ cup margarine, melted
- ⅔ cup chopped celery
- ⅔ cup chopped onion
- 2 Tbsp dried parsley flakes
- 2 packages (6 oz) cubed dried bread
- 2 eggs
- 1 tsp salt
- ½ tsp pepper
- ½-1 tsp sage
- Cut up pieces of turkey or chicken

Directions:

Mix ingredients together and bake in a 9x13 pan at 350°F for 30-45 minutes. May also cook in a slow cooker.

PECAN PIE

- 4 Tbsp butter
- 3 Tbsp flour
- 3 eggs
- 1 cup chopped pecans
- 1 cup sugar
- ¾ cup white corn syrup
- 1 tsp vanilla
- 1 unbaked 9-inch pie shell

Directions:

Preheat oven to 350°F. Cream butter with flour and sugar. Add syrup. Beat eggs together and stir in. Add vanilla. Add pecans and stir until blended. Pour into unbaked pie shell and bake at 350°F for 45 minutes. *Serves 8.*

PUMPKIN PIE

- 1 unbaked 9-inch pie shell
- 1¾ cups pumpkin
- ¾ cup sugar
- ½ tsp salt
- 1 tsp cinnamon
- ½ tsp ginger
- ¼ tsp ground cloves
- 2 eggs
- 1 (12 oz) can evaporated milk

Directions:

Preheat oven to 425°F. Combine all ingredients in a blender. Mix until smooth and pour into pie shell. Bake for 15 minutes. Reduce temperature to 350°F and bake for 40-50 minutes until knife inserted comes out clean.

COUNTRY HAYRIDE

Theme: Recognizing God's goodness in the countryside as you slowly take in all the beauty of the autumn season.

Verses to share and meditate on:

Psalm 65:8-9, *The whole earth is filled with awe at your wonders; where morning dawns, where evening fades, call forth songs of joy. You care for the land and water it; you enrich it abundantly. The streams of God are filled with water to provide the people with grain, for so you have ordained it.*

Psalm 107:31

Psalm 107:1

Psalm 27:13

Psalm 52:1

Psalm 31:19

Nahum 1:7

Romans 4:2

Start by locating someone with a tractor and hay rack filled with bales of hay who is willing to take your family and friends on a hayride in the country. Throw in lots of blankets to wrap up in if the weather is chilly. An evening hayride is nice, but afternoons are usually a little warmer if you have small children.

Some pumpkin farms offer group hayrides, so check in your area to see if that might be a possibility for you and your friends.

As you slowly tour the countryside, look around at God's goodness! In the fall the leaves turn colors. Crops are ready for harvest. Apple trees and pumpkins add rich colors to enjoy. Breathe in the brisk, fresh air and smell the scents of fall and harvest. God is so good!

Sing songs on your hayride about God's goodness to us. Kids will love to sing songs like "My God is so BIG . . . so strong and so mighty" or "God is so good."

Have a small campfire going so when you get back from the hayride, you can roast hot dogs to eat. One option would be to open cans of chili and set the cans in a heavy duty old pan filled with water. Put the pan over the open fire to warm up the chili to put on the hot dogs in a bun, and they become chili dogs! Serve chips and drink.

Make s'mores for dessert by roasting marshmallows and putting them between two graham crackers with a chunk of chocolate in the middle. Yummy!

Keep the fun going by bobbing for apples and then eating the apples. If you have children, they might need to bob with their elbows!

You might also have fun with a pumpkin carving/decorating contest for kids and adults.

RECIPES:

PUMPKIN BARS

- 2 cups flour
- ½ tsp salt
- 2 cups sugar
- 2 tsp baking powder

- 1 cup oil
- 2 tsp cinnamon
- 1 tsp baking soda
- 1 tsp ginger
- 2 cups pumpkin
- 1 tsp vanilla
- 4 eggs

Directions:

Preheat oven to 350°F. Stir together dry ingredients in a medium bowl. In a separate bowl, beat together the eggs, oil, pumpkin, and vanilla. Add dry ingredients and mix. Bake in a lightly sprayed jelly roll pan for 25 minutes. Frost.

Frosting:

- 1 large package cream cheese
- 1 stick margarine
- 1 tsp vanilla
- 3½ cups powdered sugar

Directions:

Mix together until smooth and creamy. Spread on bars.

CARAMEL FOR APPLES

- 1 cup butter or margarine
- 2¼ cups brown sugar
- Dash of salt
- 1 cup light corn syrup
- 1 (14 oz) can sweetened condensed milk
- 1 tsp vanilla

Directions:

Melt butter in heavy 3-quart saucepan. Add sugar and salt. Stir thoroughly. Stir in corn syrup; mix well. Gradually add milk, stirring constantly. Cook and stir over medium heat 12-15 minutes. Add vanilla.

BUTTERSCOTCH BROWNIES

- ¼ cup margarine
- 2 eggs, slightly beaten
- 2 cups brown sugar
- ½ cup evaporated milk
- ½ tsp salt
- 1½ cups flour
- 2 tsp baking powder
- 1 tsp vanilla
- ½ cup pecans

Directions:

Preheat oven to 350°F. Mix first 3 ingredients and then add the rest. Spread in a buttered 9x13 pan. Bake for 30-35 minutes. *Makes 15 servings.*

PEANUT BUTTER ROLO™ CUPS

- 1 package of peanut butter cookie mix
- 36 Rolos

Directions:

Prepare cookie mix according to package directions. Roll into 1-inch balls. Place balls into greased miniature muffin tins. Then press the dough into the bottom and sides of tin to form a "cup." Bake at 350°F for 11-13 minutes. Place one Rolo inside each cup immediately after removing from oven. Cool and then remove from pans. *Makes 36 treats.*

APPLE CAKE

- 2 eggs, beaten
- 2 cups sugar
- ¾ cup oil
- 4 cups apples, diced
- 1 tsp vanilla
- 2 cups flour
- 1 tsp baking powder
- 1 tsp baking soda
- 1 tsp salt
- 1 tsp cinnamon
- 1 cup pecans

Directions:

Mix first five ingredients and then add dry ingredients. Pour into a 9x13 pan and cover well with brown sugar. Bake 350°F for 45 to 60 minutes.

PROGRESSIVE DINNER

Theme: Learning and growing in Christ as we progress in our daily lives. Growth is all about change and becoming more like Christ as we read and meditate on His Word.

Verses to share and meditate on:

2 Peter 3:18, *But grow in the grace and knowledge of our Lord and Savior Jesus Christ.*

Malachi 4:2

Ephesians 4:15

1 Thessalonians 1:3

Matthew 11:29

Titus 3:14

Proverbs 1:15

Romans 15:4

A progressive dinner is fun because you get to go to different homes for each course. You also get to see and visit with different people at each stop. This type of fellowship is probably best without the kids along.

First, you will need four couples who would be willing to open their home for the evening. Usually there are four courses in a progressive dinner.

      Appetizers

      Salads

      Main Course

      Desserts

Make a sign-up sheet to pass around so participating couples can decide which part of the meal they would like to contribute to. Use paper plates and cups so there is not a lot of clean up time at each home.

A fun time to have a progressive dinner is around the Christmas season when homes are all decorated and festive. Plus, as you drive from house to house, you get to take in the Christmas lights!

Whatever course couples sign up to help with, they will need to take their contributions to that home and help the hostess serve.

Ask someone to prepare a devotional to share at the main course or dessert. It could be in relation to the Christmas season or on the theme of learning and growing in the Lord.

If you have a small group of ladies or friends, you might want to suggest a progressive eat out! Someone should choose places to stop along a particular route and call ahead to reserve tables at each restaurant. As participants stop at each restaurant, they can choose the following according to the stop:

      Drinks: Coffee/soda/tea

      First course: Garden or dinner salads

      Main Course: Sandwiches and french fries

      Dessert: Pie and/or ice cream

Enjoy your moving, changing, progressing time together!

RECIPES:

APPETIZERS

VEGETABLE PIZZA

- 1 (16 oz) can of crescent rolls
- 1 (16 oz) cream cheese
- ⅔ cup Miracle Whip™
- ¼ tsp onion salt
- ¼ tsp mustard
- 1 tsp dill weed
- ¼ tsp garlic powder
- Raw vegetables, sliced

Directions:

Spread rolls on ungreased cookie sheet. Bake at 400°F for 10 minutes. Mix remaining ingredients and spread on cooled crust. Layer vegetables-chives, mushrooms, broccoli, cauliflower, sliced radishes, shredded carrots, and green peppers. Refrigerate. *Serves 16.*

STUFFED MUSHROOMS

- ½ cup milk
- ½ cup margarine, melted
- ¾ cup Italian bread crumbs
- ⅛ to ¼ cup shredded Parmesan cheese
- Fresh mushrooms with stem removed

Directions:

Combine milk, margarine, and bread crumbs together with a fork. Fill each mushroom with mixture and top with shredded mozzarella cheese. Bake at 375°F until browned.

CRANBERRY SALSA

- 3 cups fresh cranberries (12 oz bag)
- ¼ cup minced green onion
- 2 Tbsp jalapeños minced with seeds removed
- ½ cup sugar
- ¼ cup cilantro
- 2 Tbsp finely grated ginger root
- 2 tsp lemon juice

Directions:
  Mince or chop in a food processor. Chill and serve over block of cream cheese. Serve with crackers.

PINEAPPLE CHEESE BALL

- 2 packages (8 oz) cream cheese
- ¼ cup green pepper finely chopped
- 2 Tbsp chopped onion
- 1 (8 oz) can crushed pineapple, drained
- 1 tsp seasoned salt
- ½ cup chopped pecans

Directions:
  Mix first five ingredients together in a medium-sized bowl. Refrigerate for 1 hour and then form into a ball and roll in chopped pecans.

PIZZA SQUARES

- 1 pizza crust (homemade or refrigerated package)
- 2 cups mozzarella cheese
- ⅓ cup Parmesan cheese

- ⅔ cup mayonnaise
- 2 Tbsp fresh basil, chopped
- 1 clove garlic, crushed
- 4 small tomatoes, sliced

Directions:

Preheat oven to 375°F. Roll out pizza crust on baking sheet pan. Sprinkle with 1 cup of the mozzarella cheese. Sit rest aside. Place sliced tomatoes on the crust. Mix Parmesan cheese, the remaining mozzarella, mayonnaise, basil, and garlic and scatter over the tomato layer. Spread evenly. Bake for 15-20 minutes or until crust is golden brown. Cut in squares.

GRILLED CURRIED SHRIMP

- ¼ cup olive oil
- 1 tsp coarse salt
- 1 tsp sugar
- 1 tsp curry
- ¼ tsp paprika
- 1 lb large shrimp

Directions:

Mix first five ingredients into a sauce. Then marinate shrimp in sauce for 1 hour. Grill shrimp two minutes on each side or until done.

SALADS AND BREAD

RUBY RED SALAD

- 1 can cherry pie filling
- 1 cup red raspberries

- 1 cup blueberries
- 1½ cups fresh strawberries, halved
- 1 cup red grapes, halved
- Sliced bananas, optional

Directions:

Mix all together in a serving bowl. May add bananas just before serving.

GINNY'S ROLLS

- 1 cup warm water
- 2¼ tsp yeast
- ¼ cup sugar
- ½ tsp salt
- 3 Tbsp nonfat dry milk
- 1 egg
- ⅓ cup margarine, melted

Directions:

Dissolve yeast in water and let set a few minutes. Mix together ingredients and add yeast mixture. Add 1½ cups wheat flour and beat. Then add in 2 cups white flour. Knead and place in bowl. Lightly grease top of bread with shortening. Let rise until double. Shape into rolls and bake at 350°F for 15 minutes or until golden brown.

HOMEMADE PRETZELS

- Use roll recipe from above
- ½ cup baking soda
- 4 cups hot water

Directions:

Preheat oven to 425°F. Grease cookie sheet. Dissolve baking soda in hot water. Put dough on a floured surface and divide it into 12 pieces. Roll into ropes and shape into pretzel forms.

Dip pretzels in soda solution. Sprinkle with kosher salt. Bake 8 minutes.

Cinnamon/Sugar Pretzels:

Try sprinkling the dough ropes with cinnamon and sugar before dipping them in the soda solution.

MAIN COURSE

CHICKEN AND NOODLES

Directions:

Cook a whole chicken or just the pieces you like in a big pot with 5 cups water. Cook about 30 to 45 minutes. Cool enough to pick the meat off the bones. Save chicken broth to cook the noodles in. You may need to add extra chicken bouillon for more flavor. Bring broth to a boil and start adding noodles a few at a time so they don't clump together. Add some of the flour you rolled the noodles in to thicken the broth. Stir and turn down heat. Cook until noodles are soft. Add chicken and stir.

Homemade Noodles:

- 5 egg yolks
- 1 whole egg
- 2 cup water
- 1 tsp salt
- 3 cups flour (total)

Directions:

Mix first four ingredients together and add 1 cup flour. Add more flour, kneading until stiff. Divide dough in half. Roll out thin on floured board. Roll each half very thin in the shape of a rectangle. Cut into 3 inch strips. Place strips on top of each other with plenty of flour in between strips so they don't stick together. Start at the end and cut off the noodles. Use immediately or let dry.

SCALLOPED POTATOES AND HAM

- ½ cup butter
- ½ cup flour
- 2 tsp salt
- ½ tsp pepper
- 3 cups milk
- 3 cups ham, cooked
- 1 large onion, chopped
- ½ cup cheddar cheese, shredded
- 5 cups potatoes, pared and sliced

Directions:

Melt butter in large sauce pan over low heat; blend in flour, salt, and pepper. Cook, stirring constantly, for about 1 minute. Remove from heat gradually stir in milk. Return to heat; cook until thickened and bubbly. Fold in ham, onion, and cheese. Pour over potatoes in a large bowl. Stir gently and then move into a buttered 9x13 inch baking dish; cover with foil. Bake at 350°F for 30 minutes.

Uncover and continue to bake for 1 hour. Let stand for 10 minutes before serving.

DESSERTS

CREAM PUFF DESSERT

- 1 cup water
- 1 stick margarine
- 1 cup flour
- 4 eggs
- 1 (8 oz) package cream cheese
- 8 oz Cool Whip™
- 1 package instant vanilla pudding
- 3 cups milk
- Hershey's™ chocolate syrup

Directions:

Boil water and margarine together. Add flour and eggs (eggs one at a time). Stir all together with a fork. Put in greased 10x15 glass baking dish. Bake 20 minutes at 400°F. Cool.

Mix milk, cream cheese, and dry pudding mix. Pour over cooled crust. Spread Cool Whip over pudding. Drizzle chocolate syrup over the top. With a knife, cut through syrup to decorate just before serving. *Makes 12 servings.*

CHOCOLATE CHIP CHEESECAKE

Crust:

- 2 cups vanilla wafer crumbs
- 1 cup flaked coconut, toasted
- ½ cup finely chopped pecans
- ¼ cup sugar
- 3 Tbsp cocoa
- ⅓ cup melted butter

Filling:

- 4 (8 oz) packages cream cheese, softened
- 1 cup sugar
- 4 Tbsp corn starch
- 4 eggs
- ⅓ cup whipping cream
- 3 tsp vanilla
- 1½ cups miniature semi-sweet chocolate chips

Topping:

- 3 (1 oz) squares semi-sweet chocolate melted
- 1 Tbsp margarine, melted
- 1 cup powdered sugar
- ¼ cup whipping cream

Directions:

In a bowl, combine the first 5 ingredients. Stir in butter. Press into the bottom and up the sides of a 10-inch spring form pan. Refrigerate for 15 minutes.

In a mixing bowl, beat cream cheese until smooth. Combine sugar and cornstarch and beat into the cream cheese mixture. Add eggs and beat on low speed until combined. Add the whipping cream, vanilla, and chocolate chips. Pour into crust.

Place pan on a baking sheet and bake at 350°F for 60-65 minutes. Carefully run knife along the edge to loosen. Cool for 1 hour.

For the topping, combine chocolate, butter, and sugar. Slowly beat in cream cheese until the batter is spreadable. Spread over cheesecake. Refrigerate overnight and then remove from pan.

For more information about

Dee Travis

and
Celebrate Life!
please visit:

dtravis56@wildblue.net
www.facebook.com/DeeTravis

For more information about
AMBASSADOR INTERNATIONAL
please visit:

www.ambassador-international.com
@AmbassadorIntl
www.facebook.com/AmbassadorIntl